Young**Writers** 20

PLAYGROUND

Let your creativity flow...

ode
limerick
haiku
rhyme
ballad

# Central Scotland

Edited by Laura Rogers

 Young**Writers**

First published in Great Britain in 2005 by:
Young Writers
Remus House
Coltsfoot Drive
Peterborough
PE2 9JX
Telephone: 01733 890066
Website: www.youngwriters.co.uk

SB ISBN 1 84602 182 0

# Foreword

Young Writers was established in 1991 and has been passionately devoted to the promotion of reading and writing in children and young adults ever since. The quest continues today. Young Writers remains as committed to the fostering of burgeoning poetic and literary talent as ever.

This year's Young Writers competition has proven as vibrant and dynamic as ever and we are delighted to present a showcase of the best poetry from across the UK. Each poem has been carefully selected from a wealth of *Playground Poets* entries before ultimately being published in this, our thirteenth primary school poetry series.

Once again, we have been supremely impressed by the overall high quality of the entries we have received. The imagination, energy and creativity which has gone into each young writer's entry made choosing the best poems a challenging and often difficult but ultimately hugely rewarding task - the general high standard of the work submitted amply vindicating this opportunity to bring their poetry to a larger appreciative audience.

We sincerely hope you are pleased with our final selection and that you will enjoy *Playground Poets Central Scotland* for many years to come.

# Contents

Dean Jack  (10)  13
Ryan Weaver  (10)  13

## Chapelgreen Primary School, Kilsyth
Melissa Dickinson  (9)  14
Scott Provan  (9)  14
Johanne Thornton  (10)  15
Grant Mooney  (10)  15
Craig Thomson  (10)  16
Steven Malcolm  (10)  16
Stuart Thomson  (10)  16
Jack Hannah  (10)  17
Stacey Gilmour  (11)  17
Jamie Smith  (10)  17
Keri Loudon  (10)  18
Ashleigh Meudell  (11)  18

## Colgrain Primary School, Helensburgh
Austin Gillies  (8)  18
Jay Feeney  (8)  19
Ewan Fraser  (8)  19
Tony Henderson  (8)  19
Jake Pazio  (8)  20
Calum McNeill  (8)  20
Zoe Perfect  (8)  21
Lewis Hutchison  (8)  21
Callum Robertson  (8)  21
Laura Clarke  (7)  22
Scott MacGregor  (8)  22
Sophie Maughan  (8)  22
Jasmine Daniels  (8)  23
Christopher Fagan  (8)  23
Kelsey Pearson  (8)  23
Hayley Burgin  (8)  24

## Goldenhill Primary School, Clydebank
Harry White  (11)  24
David Church  (11)  24
Eilidh Mitchell  (11)  25
Holly Munn  (11)  25

Scott Ramsay  (11)                               26
Thomas Bowie  (10)                               26
Gemma Jardine  (11)                              27
Corey Reilly  (11)                               27
Emma Stewart  (11)                               28
Greg Whyte  (11)                                 28
Madeleine Brown  (10)                            29
Thomas Blair  (11)                               29


## Greenhills Primary School, East Kilbride

Danielle Tallon  (10)                            30
Darren McConnell  (11)                           31
Lauren Boll  (10)                                32
Jenna Taylor  (11)                               32
Scott MacMillan  (11)                            33
Scott McCulloch  (9)                             33
Ashleigh Lynn  (11)                              34
Amy Milne  (10)                                  35
Lewis Deans  (11)                                36
Lisa McCulloch  (11)                             37
Jemma Parfery  (11)                              38
Amanda Brown  (8)                                38
Danielle McCann  (11)                            39
Andrew Chapman  (6)                              39
Steven O'Neill  (11)                             40
Thomas McNab  (8)                                40
Carrieann Smith  (11)                            41
Joseph Smith  (7)                                41
Iain Abernethy  (11)                             42
Michelle Fisher  (8)                             42
Megan McIntyre  (11)                             43
Kayleigh McMahon  (8)                            43
Jordan Campbell  (11)                            44
Holly Binnie  (11)                               45
Luke Quigley  (11)                               46
Ainsley Johnston  (11)                           47
Hayley Frier  (11)                               48
Craig Smith  (11)                                49
Mark MacDonald  (11)                             50
Marc McInulty  (11)                              51
Jordan McAulay  (11)                             52

## Harestanes Primary School, Kirkintilloch

| | |
|---|---|
| Jennifer Semple  (8) | 52 |
| Lucy Sinclair  (8) | 53 |
| Craig Donald  (8) | 53 |
| Ross Docherty  (8) | 54 |
| Andrew Kirkwood  (8) | 54 |
| Kerri Sinclair  (8) | 55 |
| Laura Taylor  (8) | 55 |

## High Blantyre Primary School, Glasgow

| | |
|---|---|
| Lauren Cuthbert  (9) | 55 |
| Stephen John Lappin  (9) | 56 |
| Jason Cochran  (9) | 56 |
| Scott McKean  (9) | 56 |
| Mitchell Kinnen  (9) | 57 |
| Janey Watson  (9) | 57 |
| Ross Kerr  (9) | 58 |
| Kyle Minto  (9) | 58 |
| Christopher Britton  (9) | 58 |
| Robert McKain  (9) | 59 |
| Caitlin MacLellan  (9) | 59 |
| Kimberly Black  (9) | 59 |
| Ryan McKenzie  (10) | 60 |
| Rachel Breen  (9) | 60 |
| Gordon Clark  (9) | 60 |
| Courtney Timlin  (9) | 61 |
| Dawn Thomson  (9) | 61 |
| Andrew Crombie  (9) | 61 |
| David Strain  (9) | 62 |
| Andrew Roy  (9) | 62 |
| Hannah Geddes  (9) | 62 |
| Emma McLaughlan  (9) | 63 |
| William McBride  (9) | 63 |
| Nicole Dick  (10) | 63 |
| Nicola Watson  (7) | 64 |
| Michael Reed  (9) | 64 |
| Colin Russell  (8) | 64 |
| Emma Druggan  (8) | 65 |
| Conor Cooper  (9) | 65 |

## Hills Trust Primary School, Glasgow

| | |
|---|---:|
| Jamie Low  (10) | 65 |
| Ross McMahon  (11) | 66 |
| Deborah Mulholland  (11) | 66 |
| Rhoda McKechnie  (9) | 67 |
| Calvin Borland  (9) | 67 |
| Bobby Morrell  (9) | 67 |
| Lauren Gracey  (9) | 68 |
| Amin Fayaz  (10) | 68 |
| Kimberly Ferguson  (9) | 68 |
| Chelsea Mills  (9) | 68 |
| Chelsea Geddes  (9) | 69 |
| Michael McKechnie  (8) | 69 |
| Emma McLachlan  (8) | 69 |
| Erin Armstrong  (8) | 69 |
| Christopher Mills  (11) | 70 |
| Luke Burring  (7) | 70 |
| Dylan Kerr  (7) | 70 |
| Derek Bowden  (6) & Matthew MacGregor  (7) | 71 |
| Muskan Saigal  (6) & Lauren McCormick  (7) | 71 |
| Anna Tinarwo  (6) | 71 |
| Abdikarim Adan  (7) | 71 |
| Beccy Webster  (9) | 72 |
| Sean McManus  (11) | 72 |
| Connie Douglas  (11) | 73 |
| Tyla Young  (10) | 73 |
| Jacob Duncan Atkinson  (7) | 73 |

## Houston Primary School, Houston

| | |
|---|---:|
| Erin Armstrong  (9) | 74 |
| Duncan Webb  (9) | 74 |
| Kelly McGarvey  (9) | 75 |
| Michael Love  (9) | 75 |
| Mark Yuill  (9) | 76 |
| Beth Haughan  (9) | 76 |
| Katie McCowan  (9) | 77 |
| Rebecca Greenaway  (9) | 77 |
| Michael Bonner  (9) | 78 |
| Cameron Brown  (9) | 78 |
| Katie McKinlay  (9) | 79 |
| Louise Calderwood  (9) | 80 |

| | |
|---|---|
| Hannah Thomson  (9) | 80 |
| Ruairidh Fitzpatrick  (9) | 81 |
| Hannah Corr  (9) | 81 |
| Josh Penman  (9) | 82 |
| Erin Murray  (9) | 82 |
| Stephen Hedges  (10) | 83 |
| Andrew Campbell  (9) | 83 |
| Kirsten Robertson  (8) | 84 |
| Beth Gormley  (9) | 84 |
| Laura McNeill  (9) | 85 |
| Grant Cadden  (9) | 85 |
| Struan Grant  (9) | 86 |
| Tomas Canning  (9) | 87 |
| Scott Murphy  (9) | 87 |

## Killermont Primary School, Bearsden

| | |
|---|---|
| Anna Weaver-Sharpe  (9) | 87 |
| Clara Mitchell  (8) | 88 |
| Kenneth Vickers  (9) | 88 |
| Peter Thorpe  (9) | 88 |
| Yi Fei Yang  (9) | 89 |
| Harley Smith  (9) | 89 |
| Beth Trodden  (9) | 89 |
| Robbie Pollock  (9) | 89 |
| Colin Malaney  (9) | 90 |
| Josh Sorbie  (9) | 90 |
| Farah Sadiq  (9) | 90 |
| Lucy Liveston  (9) | 91 |
| Sam McLean  (9) | 91 |
| Daniel Keller  (9) | 91 |
| Grant Halley  (9) | 91 |
| Fiona Mackenzie  (9) | 92 |
| Karen Heaney  (9) | 92 |
| Jack Byrne  (9) | 92 |
| Jessica Greenhalgh  (9) | 93 |
| Sarah Hooper  (9) | 93 |
| Maighdlin Gold  (9) | 93 |
| Eric Corson  (9) | 94 |
| Rachael Horne  (9) | 94 |
| Connor Galbraith  (9) | 95 |

## St Thomas' Primary School, Neilston

| | |
|---|---|
| Harry Hogan (10) | 152 |
| Matthew Gallanagh (9) | 153 |
| Marianne Gallanagh (11) | 153 |
| Katie Mackenzie (9) | 154 |
| Megan McCarron (9) | 154 |
| Jack Mayberry (11) | 154 |
| Amy Smith (11) | 155 |
| Melissa Linda McGlinchey (11) | 155 |
| Dennis Sweenie (11) | 156 |
| Susanne Wallace (11) | 156 |

## St Timothy's Primary School, Greenfield

| | |
|---|---|
| Christopher Allen (11) | 157 |
| Iona May (11) | 157 |
| Kieran Gibbens (9) | 158 |
| Laura Henaghen (11) | 158 |
| Shannon Love (11) | 159 |
| James Reynolds (11) | 159 |
| Hannah Neilson (11) | 160 |
| Steven Slane (9) | 160 |
| Chloe O'Donnell (11) | 160 |
| Kieran Regan (11) | 161 |
| Anthony Canning (11) | 161 |
| Chantelle McMillan (11) | 161 |
| Pauline Clark (11) | 162 |
| Kayleigh McGuirk (11) | 162 |
| Michael McCann (11) | 162 |
| Kierron McArthur (11) | 163 |
| Carly Docherty (11) | 163 |
| Kieran Donaldson (11) | 163 |
| Ryan Clifford (11) | 164 |

## Scotstoun Primary School, Scotstoun

| | |
|---|---|
| Chloe Anne White (10) | 164 |
| Alexander Calderwood (10) | 165 |
| Andrew Hardie (10) | 165 |
| Conor Clements (10) | 165 |
| Rachel Turner (10) | 166 |
| Raymond Robertson (10) | 166 |
| Kieran Stewart (10) | 166 |
| Eilidh Anne Macleod (10) | 167 |

Megan Wilkie  (10)                         167
Megan Auld  (10)                           168
Lauren Walsh  (10)                         168
Amy Maclellan  (10)                        168
John-Ross Rennie  (10)                     169
Eilidh Fletcher  (10)                      169
Conor Mellish  (10)                        169
Matthew Mouat  (10)                        170
Jay Jenkins  (10)                          170
Callum McDonald  (10)                      170

## Thorntree Primary School, Glasgow
Nicole Follen  (9)                         171
Stephen Wells  (10)                        171
Karyn Ross  (9)                            172
John Sneddon  (10)                         172
Roxanne Wright  (10)                       172
Amy Higgins  (10)                          173
Nicole McIntosh  (10)                      173
Kyle Harris  (10)                          173
James Paterson  (9)                        174
Daniel Melrose  (10)                       174
Ali Sedgwick  (10)                         174
Kimberley McCarron  (10)                   175

# The Poems

# Snow

When snow falls silvery-white
The little robin sings
A sweet calming song.
After the snowball fight
All there is left
Are footprints in the snow.
Soft, cold powder-like snowflakes
On a wintry, windy day.
Lots of children are excited,
Falling, slowly the fragile snowflakes
Are drifting down to Earth.
The trees are coldly dangling
Their branches to the rhythm
Of the snowflakes falling.
Santa Claus is flying
Through the sky.
All that snowy owls do
Is hoot through the night.

**Siobhan Wallace  (9)**
**Alexandra Parade Primary School, Dennistoun**


# Winter

Winter comes once a year,
Slippy ice to make you fear.
Snow falling all around,
Lightly scattered on the ground.
Winds howling through the night,
It blows so hard you get a fright.
Rain lashing hard and fast,
Hopefully this won't last.
Christmas time is at the end of the year,
Cakes and buns and Christmas cheer.

**Chloe McKenzie  (9)**
**Alexandra Parade Primary School, Dennistoun**

# Wintry Snow

Lovely cold icy snowflakes
That are shaped just like stars.
They dance as they land on streets.
Kids fool around having snowball fights.
Little robin freezing to death.
Little robin singing a song all alone.

Trees cold and bare and freezing.
Tree branches are snapping.
The tree trunks are snapping.
Children making snow angels.
Children are sledging down hills.
Children making snowmen.

Footprints in the snow.
No more kids on the streets.
Children shouting, 'Santa!'
Children open their presents.
Children enjoying their presents.
Children are very tired.

Streets are quiet now.
People having Christmas dinner.
Kids are watching Christmas cartoons.
Kids are asleep now.

**Jack Fox  (9)**
**Alexandra Parade Primary School, Dennistoun**


# Fairy Dust

Fairy dust, fairy dust,
Makes you fly,
You might even want to fly to the sky.
Fly over the rooftops, fly, just fly.

**Jade Sawers  (11)**
**Arden Primary School, Glasgow**

# Chick My Moves

Once I had a little friend,
His name was Chick
Then Chick had a song
And it went like this:

I might be small, I might be sweet
But baby I sure know how to move my feet . . .
Hit it.
My friend is Garry he's taken care of me,
That's a friend, and a friend for me.

**Garry Argo (11)**
**Arden Primary School, Glasgow**


# Freezy Day

Today it's freezing cold, showery and Baltic.
It is a cold day.
I wish it was sunny.
It's only sunny at the weekend.
It's shocking, I wish it was sunny
Every day of the year.

**David McCracken (11)**
**Arden Primary School, Glasgow**


# Time For School

Cereal in my shoes!
Jam in my *socks!*
Toast in my trouser pocket!
Now I'm off to school!

**Shaun Duff (11)**
**Arden Primary School, Glasgow**

# Happiness

Happiness is a lovely orange colour
It makes me happy.

Happiness is a cup of hot chocolate
In my hand.

Happiness sounds like birds chirping.

Happiness smells like a home cooked meal.

Happiness looks like a sun setting at night.

Happiness feels like a beautiful soft cover.

**Nicole Leggatt (11)**
**Arkleston Primary School, Renfrew**

# Love

Love is the colour of a big red juicy love heart,
Love tastes like a milk chocolate cake,
Love smells of a strawberry milkshake,
Love looks like shooting stars,
Love sounds like birds twittering in the air,
Love feels like a red fluffy pillow.

**Rachel Manning (11)**
**Arkleston Primary School, Renfrew**

# Anger

Anger is a misty, dark black night in the middle of nowhere,
Anger is the nasty taste of sand,
Anger is milk out of date,
Anger is the hard waves in the sea bashing at the rocky edge,
Anger is a band smacking their drum,
Anger is a rough surface on a rock.

**Paul Povah (11)**
**Arkleston Primary School, Renfrew**

# Depression

Depression is a dark grey cloud in the sky,
Depression is the taste of a very sour apple,
Depression is the smell of socks that have not been washed,
Depression is the look of the rainy dark sky,
Depression is the sound of the thunder in the sky,
Depression is the feeling that you want to kill yourself.

**Dale Hutchison  (11)**
**Arkleston Primary School, Renfrew**


# Pop Singer

I can hear people singing with me,
I can hear myself singing,
I can hear people shouting at me,
I can see lots of people jumping up and down,
I can see Mum and Dad, very happy for me,
I can see the door opening,
I can feel fear in my heart,
I feel my stomach turning,
I feel scared.

**Heather McCallum  (12)**
**Auchinloch Primary School, Auchinloch**


# The Boy Playing

As the boy played in the sand
The sun was beating down on his hand.
As he jumped about in the sea,
Water was splashing around his knee.

Sharks were swimming in the sea,
The boy he turned and started to flee,
Just as he shouted out to his mum,
The shark bit him on the *bottom!*

**Stephen Glasgow  (11)**
**Auchinloch Primary School, Auchinloch**

# War And Fear

Trembling with fear,
A soldier am I,
A worried tear,
Falling from my eye.

Bombing and gunshot!
I'm ready to die,
All we've been taught,
Can't give up, I sigh.

Lying on the ground,
Got to carry on,
The deafening sound,
So tired, I yawn.

A shiver so cold,
The rain's begun,
'Stay there,' I'm told,
With the shot of a gun.

But soon I get it into my head,
With a cry, a call, a yell or a shout,
My eyes so cold, my mouth so dead,
That's what a soldier in war's all about.

**Jennifer King (11)**
**Auchinloch Primary School, Auchinloch**


# A Day In A Game!

I was sucked into a game,
I could see sand creatures and the Dahaka,
It's black like a black hole,
It sounds like thunder blasting in the air
It tastes like salty water in my throat,
It reminds me of getting slashed in the eye.

**Calum Hetherwick (10)**
**Auchinloch Primary School, Auchinloch**

# Tiger

Prowling round and round,
Without a single sound.
Did you see that twitch?
Did you see that ditch?
Did you feel that tingle,
Just that little mingle?

Here guys, I see some food,
Just over in that wood.
It looks yum, yum, yum,
And as ready as a plum.
Did you hear that bang?
Must be hunter's gang.

Everyone run, they're coming
With their guns, *watch out!*
Oh no, he's dead without a doubt.
Can you see that dark wood?
We'll hide there, understood?

It's safe, they're gone
Now that the sun has shone.
It's time for a little nap.
Just watch out for all those traps!

**Kayleigh Eskdale (10)**
**Auchinloch Primary School, Auchinloch**

# A Day As A Spitfire!

Houses on fire is what I desire,
The noise of screaming is what I hear,
People running, I can see!
*Ta-ra-rara,*
The feeling of bullets off my scale,
I swoop down for the kill.
I feel I'll never eat again.

**Jack Lewis (10)**
**Auchinloch Primary School, Auchinloch**

# Everywhere

Silence everywhere,
Not a sound,
Not even a whisper,
To tell me I'm safe.

Darkness everywhere,
Not a light,
Not even a twinkling star,
To guide me to the light.

Loneliness everywhere,
Not a friend,
Not even a soul,
To show me the way.

**Karina Wilson  (11)**
**Auchinloch Primary School, Auchinloch**


# War

I'm a tall soldier going to war
I'm dreading it!
I'm tired and not feeling comfortable.
There are tears running down my face.
The bumping of the engine is making me feel sick.
I'm frightened I'm going to lose my life.
I feel cold goosebumps on my arms.
The smoky environment is sickening.
I can see people rattling with things,
And others lighting up cigarettes,
One after the other.

**Ashley O'Connor  (11)**
**Auchinloch Primary School, Auchinloch**

# War

A pilot flying in the air
The pilots flying behind him are scared.
He can hear jets getting shot out of the air.
A jet just clips him,
He loses control, he flies out of the sky,
Ejects just in time,
Then he can see and hear his jet explode.

**Scott Grant  (10)**
**Auchinloch Primary School, Auchinloch**

# War

In the war there are guns firing and fighter planes,
Our guns are fast. Faster than a turbo blast.
The planes can beat 150 children.
I can feel the ejector button.
In my plane I am firing back at my enemy,
Trying to shoot me.
I hear bombs flying by me.

**Dean Rigley  (10)**
**Auchinloch Primary School, Auchinloch**

# War Pilot

I can hear the jet roaring
I can see the blue sky getting darker,
The clouds were funny looking,
I can feel the jet shaking around,
I can smell the flames from my teammate's jet,
It has been shot at, this reminds me of fear.

**Lewis Marshall  (11)**
**Auchinloch Primary School, Auchinloch**

# War

In the middle of the North Sea,
Sailing to Germany.
Soldiers on deck
Ready to depart
On the coast of Germany.
Soldiers running about,
Shouting, some nervous.
Planes flying high
Hearing their engines
Making a racket.
The water's waves turning the boat wheel
Feeling seasick from all the waves
Noise of tanks on deck
Ready to go when the captain says.

**Billy Devine  (10)**
**Auchinloch Primary School, Auchinloch**


# War Pilot

I hear
The roar of the engines either side of me.
The guns of enemy planes far behind me.

I feel
My cold hands on the steering wheel.
The cold glass of my goggles against my skin.

I see
The foggy sky ahead.
The other planes around me.

Oh no, enemy aircraft ahead.

**Lewis Macleod  (11)**
**Auchinloch Primary School, Auchinloch**

# Evacuation

Standing, shaking,
Scared and nervous.
Gripping my mother's hand.
Heart is pounding,
Anxious, breathless.
Leaving my mother's side.
Tears are streaming
Children screaming
All my happiness died.

Train is leaving
Children waving
Emotions running high.
Doors are slamming
Whistle blowing
Trying not to cry.
Wheels are rushing
Smoke is puffing
Fields are flashing by.

Journey's ending
Train is slowing
Screeching to a halt.
People standing
Waiting, searching
Doors are opening wide.
New beginnings
Hope is rising
Now I see the light
Could it be, could it be, I will be chosen tonight?

**Laura Morrison  (11)**
**Auchinloch Primary School, Auchinloch**

# Hate

Hate is red like blood shooting
Out of your skin,
It feels like hard rocks,
Hate reminds me of fear,
Hate sounds like banging at two
In the morning,
It tastes like fire in your body,
It smells like bin bags over your head,
It looks like someone dying,
Hate feels like rocks crashing off your head.

**Thomas Milliken  (10)**
**Barlanark Primary School, Barlanark**


# Hate

Hate is black like the darkness.
It tastes like blood in the river Nile.
It smells like burning hot lava.
It looks like a raging bulldog.
It feels like being stabbed in the back.
It reminds me of when my gran died.
It sounds like rage erupting.

**Christopher Adams  (10)**
**Barlanark Primary School, Barlanark**


# Anger

Anger is crimson like blood spurting from a volcano
Anger is a blood bag empty of blood
Anger feels like a knife stabbing through your heart
Anger reminds me of nits on your head biting away
Anger tastes like a punch on the mouth.

**Jordan Dunn  (10)**
**Barlanark Primary School, Barlanark**

# Sadness

Sadness is the colour dark blue
Just like a really dull, dark day,
Sadness feels like hard rocks hitting your head,
It sounds like tears dripping out of my eyes
Into the fire,
It tastes like the sour, salty sea that hits off
The dirty rocks,
Sadness smells like the dirty washing in your kitchen,
Sadness reminds me of the day I was sick
And was very ill.

**Tamlyn Stout (10)**
**Barlanark Primary School, Barlanark**


# Sadness

Sadness is blue like tears coming out of your eyes.
It smells like my dog Whippit.
It looks like a wee guy crying.
It feels like falling forward in the pool.
It reminds me of a gerbal called Toffee.
It sounds like people crying.
It tastes like onions.

**Dean Jack (10)**
**Barlanark Primary School, Barlanark**


# Fear

Fear is black like a velvet cloak,
It reminds me of a scream,
It sounds like a gunshot,
It tastes like dry blood,
It smells like rotting eggs,
It looks like cyclops,
It feels like a jagged ball.

**Ryan Weaver (10)**
**Barlanark Primary School, Barlanark**

# Achievement

A lways aim high and never sigh
C elebrate your dreams
H old on tight to them
I gnore what others say
E ven if your dreams are wilting
    Build them up
    Keep them strong
V ery many people try to put you down
E ven if your dreams are wilting,
    Build them up
    Keep them strong
M y dreams are mighty and so are yours
E ven if your dreams are wilting
    Build them up
    Keep them strong
N obody can say your dreams are silly
T ake your dreams, they're best, so follow your quest.

**Melissa Dickinson  (9)**
**Chapelgreen Primary School, Kilsyth**


# Achievement

A chievements that the soldiers made
C elebrating the success
H aving to sacrifice lives
I nvasion
E nd of suffering soon I hope
V ictory for us
E xcellent at fighting we were
M emories we'll never forget
E nemies we fought
N ever going to happen again I hope
T errible ending.

**Scott Provan  (9)**
**Chapelgreen Primary School, Kilsyth**

# The Black Panther

The panther is soft, his jet-black fur shines in the sun.
He hides in the trees and watches for his prey.
Shows his snow-white, razor-sharp teeth.
Jumps down and spreads out his killer claws.
He lands softly on his bright pink pads,
Stalking his prey.
Bites into it with his teeth, as sharp as razors.
One bite can kill.
His eyes glow like burning fires.
Night falls, he creeps back to his high tree.
Lies down and sleeps till next morning.

**Johanne Thornton  (10)**
**Chapelgreen Primary School, Kilsyth**


# The Bear

The bear's fur is fluffy and warm,
Until he jumps in the water.
His claws as lethal as razor blades,
To scare away predators that threaten him or his family.
His teeth are as sharp as saws moving back and forth
                                        to rip fish apart,
Then he swallows it like a smoothie.
A boy approaches his cubs,
The bear stands up on his hind legs and roars as loud as a lion.
The boy runs.
The powerful bear has succeeded to scare the boy away.

**Grant Mooney  (10)**
**Chapelgreen Primary School, Kilsyth**

# The Wind

The howling wind darts through the trees.
Howling like a wolf and moving as fast as a lion.
The wind has a fiery temper like lava.
Wind can cause destruction and devastation,
Accidents happen like the click of my fingers.
But sometimes we need the wind,
On a boiling hot summer's day,
When we get too hot we rely on the wind.
It is as fierce as a volcano's eruption.
The wind is invisible but you can feel its power.
The power that can thrash a massive cargo ship.
The wind has a temper so keep it happy.

**Craig Thomson (10)**
**Chapelgreen Primary School, Kilsyth**


# The Wolf

The wolf fast and deadly.
Teeth strong as steel,
Claws sharp as razors.
Brave as a lion.
Its coat is wiry,
A wolf pack can kill anything.
It sneaks up on its prey,
Can kill in a heartbeat.

**Steven Malcolm (10)**
**Chapelgreen Primary School, Kilsyth**


# Fear

Fear is as dark as the night sky,
It sounds like the evil laughter of the Devil,
It feels like sharp daggers in your sides.
Fear can kill with its evil ways,
Fear is demonic.

**Stuart Thomson (10)**
**Chapelgreen Primary School, Kilsyth**

# The Wind

At night I lie awake,
Listening to the sounds of the wind.
As the wind howls I wonder what sounds I might hear,
It sounds like a steam train,
As it rattles across the track,
Invisible yet powerful.
Sometimes it can be gentle,
A nice cooling breeze when I am as hot as a cooker,
I feel like I am flying when the wind blows past my face.
If you want to keep the breeze, don't insult the wind.

**Jack Hannah (10)**
**Chapelgreen Primary School, Kilsyth**

# The Wind

The wind has two moods.
Wind screeches like a banshee,
As fast as a bullet train.
Powerful as a grown black bear.
Fierce as a tiger looking for its prey.
A hurricane clears everything in its way.
A gentle summer breeze cooling us down.
Trees sway like rocking chairs going mad.
Leaves twirl and twist in its path.
It is a threat to everyone and everything.

**Stacey Gilmour (11)**
**Chapelgreen Primary School, Kilsyth**

# The Eagle

The king of the sky
It moves as fast as lightning
Its yellow eyes look at its prey
He grabs his prey with his sharp deadly claws.

**Jamie Smith (10)**
**Chapelgreen Primary School, Kilsyth**

# Snow

Snow is like a white, glittering carpet lying all over the ground.
Snowflakes twist and turn like ballerinas fluttering
*Down, down, down.*
Children make snowmen with long carrot noses and dark coal eyes
A heavy blue scarf round his neck, an old top hat on his head.
When you go sledging you get chills on your face.
Cars get icy windows, forming a lovely pattern.
Doors get stiff, hard to open
When snow starts to melt we know the lovely white, glittering carpet
has gone forever.

**Keri Loudon (10)**
**Chapelgreen Primary School, Kilsyth**


# The Wind

The wind can be very fierce
Leaves twirl and twist everywhere
It's as powerful as a full grown black bear
It howls as loud as a wolf
As fierce as a tiger attacking its prey
The wind is as fast as a bullet train
It's invisible, but you can feel its power
It makes trees sway like a baby's cradle
Respect the wind or it won't be happy.

**Ashleigh Meudell (11)**
**Chapelgreen Primary School, Kilsyth**


# The Battle

I see stones collapsing, people fainting, arrows coming.
I hear people shouting, stones rumbling, birds singing.
I am very sore, I am unhappy, I'm sad.
I wish I didn't exist.

**Austin Gillies (8)**
**Colgrain Primary School, Helensburgh**

# The Battle

I see men falling from battlements
And people falling from ladders,
I see arrows flying.

I hear loud bangs and swords clashing
And the crackling of flames.

I am scared and frightened,
I am angry.

I wish this battle had never started.

**Jay Feeney (8)**
**Colgrain Primary School, Helensburgh**


# The Battle

I see a siege tower burning and archers,
And there's a whole army in the distance.

I hear them march beyond us and the cackle of the flames,
I hear swords clash against each other.

I am enraged and shocked.
I wish these people wouldn't do this.

**Ewan Fraser (8)**
**Colgrain Primary School, Helensburgh**


# The Battle

I see arrows flying, men dying and bricks falling.
I hear people crying, men digging and the sound of bricks breaking.
I am feeling too scared to talk or shout,
moan or even open my mouth.
I wish there was no such things as battles.

**Tony Henderson (8)**
**Colgrain Primary School, Helensburgh**

## The Battle

I see arrows flying, I see sword fights,
I see people dying.

I hear blood gurgling on the floor.
I hear loud bangs.
I hear flames.

I am scared.
I am worried.
I am terrified.

I wish I was never born.
I wish I was invisible.
I wish the battle would have ended.

**Jake Pazio  (8)**
Colgrain Primary School, Helensburgh


## The Battle

I see towers with stones falling,
I see sword fights.
I see giant catapults.

I hear swords clanging.
I hear big bangs.
I hear screaming and shouting.

I feel fed up with battles.
I feel unhappy.

I wish I could go fast as lightning
And no one will notice I have gone.

**Calum McNeill  (8)**
Colgrain Primary School, Helensburgh

# The Battle

I see men falling from battlements
And men dashing from tower to tower,
Men on ladders.

I hear loud bangs from rocks falling
And the sound of flames and men's footsteps.

I am frightened and scared
My dad may die.

I wish the battle would end.

**Zoe Perfect  (8)**
**Colgrain Primary School, Helensburgh**


# The Battle

I see a burning drawbridge, arrows flying
And sword fights.
I hear swords clashing, loud bangs,
And the crackling of flames.
I am confused, sad and shocked,
I wish my mum hadn't died in the battle.

**Lewis Hutchison  (8)**
**Colgrain Primary School, Helensburgh**


# The Battle

I see men falling from the battlements
And men falling from ladders,
I see arrows flying.
I hear loud bangs and shouts to get men to retreat.
I am very, very confused, and terrified in case my dad dies.
I wish the battle would end.

**Callum Robertson  (8)**
**Colgrain Primary School, Helensburgh**

# The Battle

I see a stampede of men,
Arrows flying, wounded men.

I hear swords clashing,
Loud bangs,
The crackling of flames.

I am scared and worried.

I wish the battle had never started.

**Laura Clarke  (7)**
**Colgrain Primary School, Helensburgh**


# The Battle

I see men with axes and people getting killed
And people with swords.

I hear people screaming and shouting
And flames crackling up in the air.

I feel miserable and frightened and angry.

I wish the war had not begun.

**Scott MacGregor  (8)**
**Colgrain Primary School, Helensburgh**


# The Battle

I see men getting killed and arrows getting shot at people,
And horses getting ridden about over the battle.

I hear swords crashing
And people crying and shouting.

I feel angry and very sad.

I wish this war had never started.

**Sophie Maughan  (8)**
**Colgrain Primary School, Helensburgh**

# The Battle

I see sword fights in this battle,
All around me, every night.
I see arrows flying in the dark, all night long.
I see men getting killed by swords as the night goes on and on.
I hear enemies getting attacked in the night.
The sound of people getting killed all night long.
I feel anxious.
I wish I could stop this battle.

**Jasmine Daniels (8)**
**Colgrain Primary School, Helensburgh**


# The Battle

I see men falling and castles breaking
And dead bodies.

I hear swords crashing,
Footsteps and loud bangs.

I feel unhappy, sad and scared.

I wish the war didn't exist.

**Christopher Fagan (8)**
**Colgrain Primary School, Helensburgh**


# The Battle

I see arrows flying, giant catapults, sword fights.

I hear the clatter of rocks,
The crash of Port Cullis closing
The sound of loud bangs.

I am terrified and confused.

I wish the battle had never started.

**Kelsey Pearson (8)**
**Colgrain Primary School, Helensburgh**

# The Battle

I see giant catapults firing arrows,
A stampede of men.
I hear loud bangs, swords clashing, rocks falling.
I am confused, anxious,
I wish this battle had never started.

**Hayley Burgin (8)**
**Colgrain Primary School, Helensburgh**

# Bullying!

They walk around thinking they're the boss,
They don't realise they've got the loss.
They try to push you around,
Stand up for not just you but everyone around!

They think they're the best,
But you know they're just like the rest.
They pick on you because they've no friends,
So when your happiness starts, theirs ends!

**Harry White (11)**
**Goldenhill Primary School, Clydebank**

# School Dinners

The greasy, mushy chips
That I put in my lips.
The big pieces of cod and the peas in a pod.
Will it be cold,
Will it be hot?
Did I say hot?
I think not.
Dinnerladies, I don't mean to be rude,
But tomorrow try and make some decent food.

**David Church (11)**
**Goldenhill Primary School, Clydebank**

# The School Cleaner's Cupboard

I've never been in the school cleaner's cupboard
But I've heard it's an awful place,
Do mop men jump out at you and soak you through the skin?
Do brushes brush you away?
Does the vacuum cleaner suck you into a bag
To be thrown out the next day?

As I ventured through the busy school hall,
I came across the school cleaner's cupboard.
Would the mop men be dipping their heads in water?
Would the brushes be aiming their bristles?
Would the vacuum be sucking wildly at the door?

I opened the door and stared into the pitch-black cupboard,
Yes there were mops,
Yes there were brushes,
Yes there were vacuum cleaners,
But they all stayed completely still.

**Eilidh Mitchell  (11)**
**Goldenhill Primary School, Clydebank**


# My Best Friend

My best friend is not human,
In fact, he is a dog.
Casper is my best friend because
I know he's always there for when I am feeling down.
I know he always cares.
If I'm upset he will cheer me up,
The way he looks you in the eye,
The way he licks you on the face and wakes you in the morning.
I love it!
I care for him with all my might,
This means he'll never leave me.

**Holly Munn  (11)**
**Goldenhill Primary School, Clydebank**

# Playground Fun

P eople are running.
L ots of fun.
A nyone can join our game.
Y oung or old, whatever the age.
G oing round the roundabout.
R aces big and small.
O n your mark, get set, go!
U p and round the tree and back.
N ever wanting the fun to stop.
D on't want any work never!

F un here and fun there.
U ntil the bell goes *bring bring bring!*
N ot one of us wants to go in. *Help!*

**Scott Ramsay (11)**
**Goldenhill Primary School, Clydebank**


# Bullies

They're mean people, very mean,
They steal your lunch money,
They bully people weaker,
And they even laugh at you for no reason.

They call you names,
They beat you up,
There's no one to stop it
So we've got to do something about it.

We'll all find a way to stop it,
We'll make them never annoy us again,
Never, ever, again.

**Thomas Bowie (10)**
**Goldenhill Primary School, Clydebank**

# Zoo At Home

Fat pets, thin pets,
Odd pets, usual pets,
In my house it's like a zoo.
Dogs: I have two
Cats: I have one
Birds: I have two
And goodness knows how many fish I have!
I love my dogs, they're like my teddies.
You can hug them and love them.
Cats and birds are like monkeys.
The birds fly from room to room
And climb all over their cages.
The cat scampers from chair to chair.
When you're sitting in the living room,
Even if it's a zoo, it's a loving one,
And I love them all.

**Gemma Jardine (11)**
**Goldenhill Primary School, Clydebank**


# Cat And A Hat

I would love to see a cat wear a hat,
It would be so funny,
Just like Bugs Bunny.
I'd make a lot of money for a show,
If I could get people to go.
Make the cat do tricks,
Make them laugh all night long,
And make it sing a song.
And make tunes of our own
*That's our show.*

**Corey Reilly (11)**
**Goldenhill Primary School, Clydebank**

# My Class

My class is full of
Noisy and quiet children.
Sometimes it is irritating,
But sometimes I join in.

My worst subject is,
Let me think, I wonder,
OK, it is maths.
The worst thing in the world.

There also are some good points,
Like when someone walks over
To the sink but,
Falls on the way!

That is my class,
Can be funny,
Can be boring,
But in the end
It is *fantastic!*

**Emma Stewart  (11)**
**Goldenhill Primary School, Clydebank**


# School Bullies

The school bullies are as mean as a bear
And as smelly as a dead hare.
They pick on people that are any size.
They always steal people's lunch money and mine too.
In the cloakroom he hangs us on the highest peg by our boxers!

He comes into class and acts like an angel.
But when it comes to football all the boys will have sore toes!
Me and my pals have got a plan to see that these bullies
Run crying to their grannies!

**Greg Whyte  (11)**
**Goldenhill Primary School, Clydebank**

## Evacuation Day

The day I leave,
Today's the day I leave,
To go far, far away,
It's *evacuation day,* you see!
I get on the train and wave goodbye.
While the train trundles away out of the station,
I think about where I'm going,
Will it be nice,
Or will it not?
I finally get there.
I'm the last one to be picked.
If only you knew what it's like to be here alone.

**Madeleine Brown  (10)**
**Goldenhill Primary School, Clydebank**


## Unlucky Fellow

On a frosty midday he decided to skate as soon
As the local pond froze,
A figure of eight
Decided his fate,
Soon icicles hung from his nose.

In one final bid this brave stupid kid
Thought tiddlywinks couldn't cause harm.
He tiddled too strong,
It flew far and long
And set off the burglar alarm!

**Thomas Blair  (11)**
**Goldenhill Primary School, Clydebank**

# It Wasnae Me

No putting the dishwasher on,
Dirty dishes packed high
Bin overflowing, food lying around
Biscuit tins, no biscuits just crumbs.
It wasnae me!

Dirty cups on the desks
Leaving the light on,
Electricity bill going sky high
Not making the bed
It wasnae me!

Dirty plates on the floor from the night before
Newspaper ripped from the hamster
Left the TV on
It wasnae me!

Leaving the tap on, flood of water out the door
Toilet roll empty
Towels hanging on the floor
It wasnae me!

**Danielle Tallon  (10)**
**Greenhills Primary School, East Kilbride**

# It Wasnae Me!

Broken CDs on the bed
Mouldy bread is turning red
And clothes are falling on my head
It's like a giant avalanche
It wasnae me!

Overflowing sink
Toothpaste on the wall
And towels lying on the floor
It's like a jungle I could explore
Don't blame me anymore.

Cookie jar empty
Milk left open on the table
And the fridge door was left open
It's as if someone's come and raided the place
He did it not me!

Drawings on all four walls
Toys all over this floor
And wrappers left by the door
It's as if a caveman lived here before
It wasnae me!

**Darren McConnell (11)**
**Greenhills Primary School, East Kilbride**

# Don't Look At Me!

Dishes not washed with food stuck to it.
Tap left on, it floods everywhere like an ocean wave.
Leaving the fridge door open makes food mouldy.
Don't look at me!

Leaving all my clothes on the floor
Looks like a massive bomb has hit my room.

Bed not made, covers all over the bed
And pillows scattered on the floor.

Leaving curtains closed so the room is dark.
Don't look at me!

Losing the control for the telly makes everyone mad.
Leaving TV on makes a little voice in the house.
Make a mess, hard to move about.
Don't look at me!

**Lauren Boll (10)**
**Greenhills Primary School, East Kilbride**


# I Always Get The Blame!

Biscuits in the tin no more
Dirty dishes on the floor
And the leftovers of a snack
Making the kitchen like a messy shack
I always get the blame!

My bedroom's so messy it's like a pigsty
And there's a pile of junk sky high
Chocolate wrappers on my bed
My bedroom's also as messy as Dad's shed
I always get the blame!

In the living room, tea's been spilt like a brown tidal wave
Running down the room like murky water in a cave
I run to get a tea towel
But parents are always on the prowl
So now I have to tidy it up.

**Jenna Taylor (11)**
**Greenhills Primary School, East Kilbride**

# It Wasnae Me

Overflowing sink soaking everything
Messy room that's almost like a jungle
Curtains hanging like a monkey
It wasnae me!

Door wide open like the sky
Brother wound up trying to hit me
Brother's room is a dump
It wasnae me!

Towels left lying like dead bodies
Dirty clothes lying like sleeping bears
Bed left unmade, don't know what's in it
It wasnae me!

Toys left lying like mines
Brother's on PC turned into a PC drone
Staying up late like a bat
It wasnae me!

**Scott MacMillan  (11)**
**Greenhills Primary School, East Kilbride**


# My Burger And Chips

Burger and chips are like fun time in gymnastics.
They look like a beautiful angel from Heaven.
They sound like a tempting voice saying, 'Eat me, eat me!'
They smell like tomato sauce.
They make me feel like I might burst.
I love my delicious burger and chips!

**Scott McCulloch  (9)**
**Greenhills Primary School, East Kilbride**

# You Always Blame Me!

Coffee marks all over the unit
Feeding the cat and putting it all over the floor
Leaving the sink on and flooding the kitchen
You always blame me!

Heaps of clothes lying on the floor
A stack of shoes at the side of my bed
Leaving my bed a mess until I get in
You always blame me!

Dirt marks all over the rug
Split juice all over the couch
Losing the controls so you can't watch the telly
You always blame me!

Leaving the tap on to flood the room
Leaving towels all over the floor, so people fall
Don't drain the bath, leave it in for Dad
You always blame me!

**Ashleigh Lynn (11)**
**Greenhills Primary School, East Kilbride**

# It Wasnae Me!

Leaving fridge door open and food going mouldy.
Tap left on, water going everywhere, dishes getting another wash.
Dirty dishes getting left beside the sink, start to smell.
It wasnae me!

Bed not made, in a state.
Clothes lying all over the place.
Blinds are left closed all day till Mum enters in.
It wasnae me!

Hiding the remote so Brother cannot change the channel.
When told to sit down I jump on the sofa.
TV left on.
It wasnae me!

Towel laying on the floor, it gets all muddy.
Tap left running, bath going all hot.
Not taking plug out, Mum goes for a bath, Mum shouts, *'Amy!'*
It wasnae me!

**Amy Milne  (10)**
**Greenhills Primary School, East Kilbride**

# It Was Him!

Dirty dishes covering the surface with food everywhere.
Fridge open and the kitchen is like a block of ice.
Biscuit tin on the floor with broken biscuits everywhere.
It was him!

Drawers left open with clothes hanging out.
Sweet wrappers and half finished jigsaws on the floor.
PC on and music playing loud but I'm fast asleep.
It was him!

Magazines and papers from last month everywhere.
The TV is on but no channel is on for at least one minute.
Every day the sofas and tables are positioned in a different place.
It was him!

The taps are running and the bathroom is nearly flooded.
Toilet seat is up and it is not flushed.
Towels all over the floor and the bathroom looks multicoloured.
It was him!

**Lewis Deans  (11)**
**Greenhills Primary School, East Kilbride**

# It Was Jade

Dirty dishes overflowing in the sink.
Bin not put out, everything overflowing.
Dog food on the floor when putting it out.
It was Jade!

Not making my bed, very messy.
Room very untidy, stuff everywhere.
Not turning my light off, Dad comes and shouts.
'It was Jade!'

Leaving the tap on water going everywhere.
Towels on the floor it becomes very messy.
Leaving shower up too hot, everyone shouting that it is too hot!
It was Jade!

TV control missing under chairs.
TV left on when we are out.
Moving everything around making everyone comfy.
It was Jade!

**Lisa McCulloch (11)**
**Greenhills Primary School, East Kilbride**

# It Wasnae Me!

Leaving dirty dishes piling up like mountains of snow.
Spilling juice like a volcano splattering out.
Clothes lying on floor and creeping out of the cupboard.
CDs scattered like UFOs landing.
It wasnae me!

Leaving butter lying out to melt like big swimming pools.
Leaving fridge door open and mouldy food creeping out.
Leaving cupboard doors open like someone's new house.
It wasnae me!

Knocking washing over like a big rainbow.
Leaving glasses piling up like a bowling alley.
It wasnae me!

Leaving towels lying like a sandy beach.
Spilling water like a dog creeping out.
It wasnae me!

**Jemma Parfery (11)**
**Greenhills Primary School, East Kilbride**


# Going To Sea

All aboard we're off to sea
I am sailing with a chimpanzee
We won't be back till half past three
The sea is choppy and rough
I really don't want to bluff
It would be better on a bus
I am home at last safe and sound.

**Amanda Brown (8)**
**Greenhills Primary School, East Kilbride**

# Wasnae Me!

Clothes like a mountain lying on my bed
Scattered make-up all on the floor
Tripping over CDs like shark infested water
It wasnae me!

Sneaking sweets and biscuits
Juice like raindrops dotted on the worktops
Leaving butter out to melt
It wasnae me!

Overflowing the shower
Toothpaste like a snake in the sink
Drawing on the mirror
It wasnae me!

Flicking through the TV channels
Turning music to too loud
Drawing on the walls
It wasnae me!

**Danielle McCann  (11)**
**Greenhills Primary School, East Kilbride**


# Snow

I can see a field of daisies.
I can smell fresh and clean air.
I hear silence.
It tastes very salty like chips.
It feels bumpy like speed bumps.

**Andrew Chapman  (6)**
**Greenhills Primary School, East Kilbride**

## It Wasnae Me!

Clothes scattered about the room,
Plates piled up like a big balloon
Leaving TV on
It wasnae me!

Crisp pokes ripped and scattered about the couch
Glasses turned upside down
Toys set out like traps on the floor
It wasnae me!

Spilled juice like a waterfall
Drawers open like a garden wall
Fridge bleeping, door's not closed
It wasnae me!

Leaving towels out like a rug
Bath tap on beginning to bug
Toilet seat up!
It wasnae me!

**Steven O'Neill (11)**
**Greenhills Primary School, East Kilbride**


## My Delicious Dairy Milk

Chocolate is like a bite of Heaven.
It looks like a teddy bear you really want to cuddle.
It sounds like a voice saying, 'Come on, eat me, I know you want to.'
It smells like heavenly chocolate melting into the air.
It feels like a hug in a wrapper.
I love my devilish chocolate.

**Thomas McNab (8)**
**Greenhills Primary School, East Kilbride**

# It Wasnae Me!

Mountains of clothes filthy and clean
Scattered all over the floor.
Manky dishes on shelves and the floor.
Stereo turned up too loud.
It wasnae me!

TV on music channel of course.
Last night's dinner dishes scattered on the floor.
My toys and games lying everywhere.
It wasnae me!

Tap running like a waterfall.
Crumbs scattered all over the worktop.
Dirty tea bags going gooey beside the sink.
It wasnae me!

A sea of water fills the sink.
Dirty, wet towels heaped on the floor.
Toothpaste on the floor like a white worm.
It wasnae me!

**Carrieann Smith (11)**
**Greenhills Primary School, East Kilbride**


# Snow

I can see ice cubes and a big white sponge and some broken glass.
I can smell fresh lettuce and salty air outside.
I can hear a volcano and some people screaming.
I can taste some sour brain drops.
It feels like soft candyfloss and a fuzzy blanket.

**Joseph Smith (7)**
**Greenhills Primary School, East Kilbride**

# It Wasnae Me!

Curtains on the floor
Bin overflowing with rubbish
Toys scattered on the floor
It wisnae me.

Fridge door left open
Milk left out
Dad's pieces go hard
It wasnae me!

PC games scattered on the floor
Crisp packets under the couch
Videos in wrong places
It wasnae me.

Toothpaste on the walls
Bathwater left in the tub
Toilet roll all wet.
It just wasnae me.

**Iain Abernethy  (11)**
**Greenhills Primary School, East Kilbride**

# My Devilish Galaxy Bar

Galaxy bars are like heaven filled with creamy chocolate.
I hear choirs of angels singing, 'Hallelujah!'
I smell chocolate melting oozingly.
I feel the temptation rising up in me.
I love my devilish, forever lasting tasting chocolate.

**Michelle Fisher  (8)**
**Greenhills Primary School, East Kilbride**

# It Wasnae Me!

The TV controls go missing
The telly left on full blast
Food wrappers dumped on the floor
It wisnae me!

Leaving the cooker on and burning food
Spilled juice all over the floor
Leaving dirty dishes all over the place
It wasnae me!

Towels piled as high as a mountain
Taps left on
The bath overloaded with water
It wasnae me!

Clothes piled as high as me
All my stuff lying everywhere
Scratched CDs and DVDs all over.

**Megan McIntyre (11)**
**Greenhills Primary School, East Kilbride**


# My Doughnuts And Chocolate Sauce

Doughnuts and chocolate sauce are like happy puppies.
They look like a chocolate and sparkly sugar angel.
They sound like sizzling, chocolaty clouds raining on me.
They smell like a sugar delight with sparkly, sparkly, tasty sugar.
They make me feel I will burst to have them.
I adore my chocolate sauce and doughnuts
Because they are like little drops of heaven.

**Kayleigh McMahon (8)**
**Greenhills Primary School, East Kilbride**

# Don't Blame Me!

Kitchen a mess like a bin, cups all over the floor,
Kitchen a mess from dinner the night before,
Kitchen a mess by all the wrappers on the floor,
Don't blame me!

Bedroom like a bombsite, rats all over the place,
Bedroom like space, dark dusty dark, with no air or light,
Bedroom bright as the sun even at night because the lights
are all on,
Don't blame me!

The living room is always loud because I forget to turn the
music down
The table is never straight because it is always about the place
'Where is the control?' my mum always says
Don't blame me!

The bedroom is always flooded because of the bath
The tap is going, *drip drop*
A mess on the floor, it's me
Don't blame me!

**Jordan Campbell  (11)**
**Greenhills Primary School, East Kilbride**

# It Wasnae Me!

Dollop of fat glistening on the surface worktop like small islands,
Dishes piled high like Mount Everest.
Not cleaning up giant cookie crumbs from toast.
It wasnae me!

Leaving toenails all over the bathroom floor,
Forgetting to pick up my clothes and leave them scattered all
over the floor,
Leaving the light on so the bulb runs out.
It wasnae me!

Not picking up sweet wrappers from the wooden floor,
Making my drawers a state and not picking them up,
Leaving pyjamas heaped like a small volcano is ready to erupt.
It wasnae me!

Losing the remote in a pile of heavy cushions,
Changing the channel in the middle of a film,
Leaving cushions scattered in the living room
Like a bomb has hit it.
It wasnae me!

**Holly Binnie  (11)**
**Greenhills Primary School, East Kilbride**

# Why Do I Always Get The Blame?

*In the bathroom.*
Rivers of water running down the plughole.
The toilet seat always standing at salute.
Clouds of sprayed deodorant on the mirror.
Why do I always get the blame?

*In my living room.*
Piles of trash glued to the floor.
The remote's always hiding away somewhere.
CDs left out as if the computer's awfully decorated.
Why do I always get the blame?

*In my bedroom.*
Clothes lying on the floor as if someone's sleeping there.
Things to go in the bin but you never bother.
Videos lying out ready for a big high heel to step on it.
Why do I always get the blame?

*In the kitchen.*
Sweets are stuffed in people's mouths before dinner.
The cooker's always boiling, nearly setting the place on fire.
Either the fridge or freezer is nearly causing an ice age.
Why do I always get the blame?

**Luke Quigley (11)**
**Greenhills Primary School, East Kilbride**

# Don't Blame It On Me!

*Bedroom*
Teddies lying on their heads.
Towers of clothes scattered on the floor.
Bedcovers laying in a heap on the floor.
Don't blame it on me!

*Bathroom*
Leaving toys out as if it were a toy cupboard.
Forget bath is running and go in and it looks like big huge clouds
                                        all over the bath.
Writing on mirrors as if it were a piece of paper.
Don't blame it on me!

*Living room*
Leaving clothes about as if it were a washing basket.
School bag lying on its side with stuff coming out of it.
Not taking plates out even though it's all mouldy the next day.
Don't blame it on me!

*Kitchen*
Taking the last packet of crisps and not putting the wrapper away.
Watches, rings, toys, sweets all scattered over the worktops.
No sweeties in the tin anymore
Don't blame it on me!

**Ainsley Johnston  (11)**
**Greenhills Primary School, East Kilbride**

# Trouble

Losing remote as if it was hid in a hundred storey building.
Fighting with sister as if you are two mad wrestlers.
Leaving things around as if it was a junkyard.
It wasnae me!

Spilling juice like a little baby.
Throwing things everywhere as if it were a basketball court.
Table dirty as if a football team ran across it.
Spilling things as if a swimming team swam across the floor.
It wasnae me!

Toothpaste all over the sink like little wriggly worms.
Floor flooded like a swimming pool.
Bath pearls everywhere as if there was a food fight.
It wasnae me!

Leaving jewellery everywhere as if it were a treasure chest.
Drawing on the walls as if it were an artist's studio.
Getting the carpet dirty as if it were a swamp.
It wasnae me!

**Hayley Frier (11)**
**Greenhills Primary School, East Kilbride**

# It Wasnae Me!

Biscuits mysteriously disappearing from the tin.
Tea stains dotted along the worktops like gravy.
Cooker being left on all the time.
It wasnae me!

Bread being left out all the time and going mouldy.
Ketchup lid not been put on and left out.
Cutlery being left on the table and not in the sink.
It wasnae me!

Coco Pops scattered along the floor and people falling.
Crisps magically disappearing out of the cupboard.
Drinking milk out of the bottle and not putting the lid on.
It wasnae me!

Fridge door being left open and everything going horrible.
Freezer door being left open and everything defrosting.
And the ice cream melting and losing its fluffiness.
It wasnae me!
*OK!*

**Craig Smith  (11)**
**Greenhills Primary School, East Kilbride**

# It Wasnae Me

*Bedroom*
Scattered clothes all over the place
Toys everywhere on the floor
Big bits of torn wallpaper hidden by posters
It wasnae me!

*Kitchen*
Millions of cups on the table filled with juice
Mucky dishes in the basin
Bread lying out on the desk tops all mouldy
It wasnae me!

*Living room*
Fluffy pillows on the floor all manky
Piles of magazines on the couch and chairs
Pens and pencils left on the iron board
It wasnae me!

*Bathroom*
Toothpaste caps lying out in the sink
Forget to turn off shower and water dribbling
Piles of towels on the floor all wet and tatty
It wasnae me!

**Mark MacDonald (11)**
**Greenhills Primary School, East Kilbride**

# It Wasnae Me!

*Bedroom*
Scraps of food hiding on plate under the unmade bed,
Rotted food all over the bin, filled to the top,
Scratched games on the floor with the cases wide open.
*It wasnae me!*

*Kitchen*
Wide open fridge leaking all over the kitchen floor,
Overflowing water still running like the Indian Ocean,
Yucky, messy food on the floor like a bin heap.
*It wasnae me!*

*Living room*
Three-week-old sweetie wrappers under Dad's favourite chair,
Mum's new newspapers in the horrifying bin,
Dirty CDs on the floor like a CD dump.
*It wasnae me!*

*Bathroom*
Soaking wet towels in the frozen cold bath,
Dried shampoo all over the stained toilet,
Toothpaste on the floor as if it is invisible.
*It just wasnae me!*

**Marc McInulty  (11)**
**Greenhills Primary School, East Kilbride**

# It Wasnae Me!

Leave the fridge wide open and the food goes mouldy.
Dishes piling up in the sink and food rotting away.
Bin overflowing empty wrappers and old food everywhere.
It wasnae me!

Homework scattered all over the floor.
Room in darkness, curtains not open, bed not being made
                                                    for one year
Rubbish left all over the floor, old gum stuck to the wall.
It wasnae me!

Lost the TV control and can't watch TV.
Old crumbs lying on the couch.
Wallpaper peeling off onto the floor.
It wasnae me!

Light left on all day.
Toilet seat left up and not put down.
Dirty towels on the floor.
It wasnae me!

**Jordan McAulay  (11)**
**Greenhills Primary School, East Kilbride**


# On A Teacher's Desk

On a teacher's desk you can find,
Folders, jotters, Sellotape, staplers, pencils, pens.
Notes of people who are being a pest.
Stickers for people who are doing their best.
Chalk, chalk dusters, letters, notebooks,
Maybe even a box of tissues.
And if you just flung it all on the floor
I am sure it would make a rather big roar.

**Jennifer Semple  (8)**
**Harestanes Primary School, Kirkintilloch**

# My Cats

My cat said I look like a rat.
I ran after him, he ran in the cat flap.
He was very, very scared
He jumped and ran.
Then he went to the hospital to get a scan.

He came back home to get some milk.
Then I saw him then he spilled his milk.
He went to Grandpa's house to get some cat food
When he finished he saw a dog and he bit his tail off
So that means he is a dead cat now.

I went to get another cat - she was great
But then she was too old then she died.

**Lucy Sinclair (8)**
**Harestanes Primary School, Kirkintilloch**


# In The Teacher's Cupboard

The teacher's cupboard is full of stuff
Trays, pencils, all sorts of stuff
You never know what's hiding in there
Does she comb her hair?
Has she got sweets in a plastic container?

There's crisps everywhere
She said, 'Do I care?'
And, 'What will I wear?'

Can you imagine being a teacher
I don't worry about my career
One thing I don't want to be is a
*Teacher!*

**Craig Donald (8)**
**Harestanes Primary School, Kirkintilloch**

# Dragons

Fire dragon, fire dragon
Evilest in the world
Catch you in his hand
Burn you to a crisp.

Ice dragon, ice dragon
Freeze you to an ice pole
And lick you until you die
And chuck you out and break you.

Rock dragon, rock dragon
Crunch you up into a ball
And play football until bedtime
When he falls asleep you'll return
To your normal size.

**Ross Docherty  (8)**
**Harestanes Primary School, Kirkintilloch**


# Monsters

The monsters live in a cave up in a mountain I was told
They are as blue as a lake, as tall as a skyscraper
And have horns on their heads.

Who are they?
What are their names?
Sally or James?
How big are their feet,
Big or small?
And what language do they speak
Scottish or French or can they talk at all?
Who knows all this?
Well don't ask me, because I don't know.

**Andrew Kirkwood  (8)**
**Harestanes Primary School, Kirkintilloch**

# Ten Things My Big Sister Likes

The things she likes . . .
Scary, spooky stuff
Fantastic football
Dangly dolls
Collectible clothes
Shiny shoes
Fancy fashion
Cute kittens
Funny films
Funky friends
I'm her little sister so of course she likes me!

**Kerri Sinclair  (8)**
**Harestanes Primary School, Kirkintilloch**


# A Big Brother

Flat football
Scotland flag
Dinosaur hidden in his bag.

Smelly socks
Stinky shoes
Silver snails on his shoes.

Nokia phone
Nails in his jacket
Don't tell Mum because it makes a *racket!*

**Laura Taylor  (8)**
**Harestanes Primary School, Kirkintilloch**


# Miss Dewar

When you get bullied in the playground Miss Dewar is always there
She has her black hood on her hair
She walks around the school with her whistle on her neck
She has a lot of work to do but she will help you.

**Lauren Cuthbert  (9)**
**High Blantyre Primary School, Glasgow**

# Gran

You're like snowflakes falling on my face,
You're like grapefruit juice sour in my mouth,
You're the fluff in my jacket,
You're the feathers in my pillow,
You're like freesias blowing in the wind
You're like a river flowing in my heart,
You are happiness all around me.
You are a star watching over me when I am asleep,
You are my hero, you are my gran.

**Stephen John Lappin (9)**
High Blantyre Primary School, Glasgow

# Nacho Novo

Nacho Novo he's my favourite
Because he scores all the goals
We're walking on a Novo Wonderland!
The same as Dado Prso
He's good at scoring goals but
He's never better than
Nacho Novo.

**Jason Cochran (9)**
High Blantyre Primary School, Glasgow

# Mum

If it was not for you I would not be in this world.
You're like a shiny, silver star in the sky.
You're like a red motorbike on the road,
You make me feel great!
You're like Quavers melting in my mouth,
You're like gold reflecting in a window,
The best thing of all is that you are my mum.

**Scott McKean (9)**
High Blantyre Primary School, Glasgow

# My New Car!

My new car is really big
It even has its own wee bed
It made my mum boom out her chair!
I always laugh when I hear
She's landed on a big fat bear!

My new car has lots of room
When Michael saw it he came in
After that I took him to mine
We went into my house and
Had our dinner!

My new car is hard to steer
The wheels make noises in my ears
I always take my dad to work
His bags are so heavy I always
*Stop!*

**Mitchell Kinnen (9)**
**High Blantyre Primary School, Glasgow**


# My Pet

My pet is a cat
She's cute and fluffy
And doesn't mind being lifted
Her ball is important to her
She loves to smell my hand
And her face is so cute!
Like a daisy in the sun!
That's why I named her Daisy
She can fit in her food bowl
She loves it when you stroke her
She's the best loving cat yet.

**Janey Watson (9)**
**High Blantyre Primary School, Glasgow**

# Saturday Morning

I woke up early on a Saturday morning
I went doon stairs tea see whits fur breakfast
There wiz nohing
Bother, bother, bother
I gote ready and went tae the shop
An' I bought some Coco Pops
I wiz tired
When I got hame I hud my breakfast
And went to bed
I woke up in the afternoon and gote some lunch
Then stayed up and watched television.

**Ross Kerr  (9)**
**High Blantyre Primary School, Glasgow**


# My Favourite Car

The Maclaren F1 is my favourite car
It is the best looking motor by far
The engine is plated in gold
Every feature is a joy to behold
It outclasses the rest
By far it's the best
That's why it's my favourite car.

**Kyle Minto  (9)**
**High Blantyre Primary School, Glasgow**


# Books

Books are funny - well some others are boring
Some are about history and some rhymes
I think Goosebumps is the best,
Some are mysteries and some are annuals
But I think spelling books are the most boring in the world!

**Christopher Britton  (9)**
**High Blantyre Primary School, Glasgow**

# The Night

The night is dark
The sky is black
The moonlight shines
Telling the night-time animals to wake up
Wake up and hunt for their food
Like worms, beetles and slugs.
Then foxes can eat some rotten bananas
And eat big, black rotten oranges
But I think they most enjoy
Big, fat, delicious, juicy mice.

**Robert McKain (9)**
**High Blantyre Primary School, Glasgow**


# I Have A Friend

I have a friend called Adele, she's funny and nice.
She always helps me if I'm down and I help her.
I shout, 'Help! Help!' And she helps me.
She is always there when I need her because she's my friend.
She always comes to my house.
And always plays with me
We always play hide-and-seek, it is *so, so fun!*

**Caitlin MacLellan (9)**
**High Blantyre Primary School, Glasgow**


# Candy

Candy is rotten if you eat too much
You are very naughty, but if you eat
Fruit you will be nice and dandy
So make sure you don't eat too much candy
Candy is sweet, very sweet so don't
Eat a lot or your teeth will rot.

**Kimberly Black (9)**
**High Blantyre Primary School, Glasgow**

# Grandad

You're blue like a big blue house,
You're like the orange juice that tickles my mouth,
You're like a leather jacket, smooth as it can be,
You're like the song from 'Titanic', very sad indeed,
You're like Ibrox, where I like to be,
You're like the steak pie that tickles my throat,
I am excited when I see you,
The world is good but it could be better with you.

**Ryan McKenzie  (10)**
**High Blantyre Primary School, Glasgow**


# Mrs Black

If yir oot in the playground an ye have a wee trip
If ye grazed yir knee or yir dress has a rip
Mrs Black will tak ye in an say 'Dinna you fret'
She'll even gie ye a dress if yirs is aw wet

Noo oot in the playground where the girls chat
The boys run aroon an act like a bat!
Mrs Black will patrol an walk roon an roon
I'll tell ye nae mare fir she's comin' roon soon!

**Rachel Breen  (9)**
**High Blantyre Primary School, Glasgow**


# My Best Friend Andrew

My best friend Andrew is as fast as a hare
But when he's mad, stay well away!
He'll chase you round the playground
When you're playing tig - beware, you're in for a scare.

**Gordon Clark  (9)**
**High Blantyre Primary School, Glasgow**

# Kelly

You're terrific, always happy,
You're pink, just the way I like you,
You make me laugh and giggle,
You remind me of a fox, always ready to go.
You're a quiet tune in my ears,
You're Irn-Bru, fizz-pop in my mouth,
You're great, you're fantastic!
You feel like denim,
Don't ever, ever change.

**Courtney Timlin (9)**
**High Blantyre Primary School, Glasgow**


# Penny

You're as sweet as the colour pink,
You're like the gravy on my chips,
You're the chocolate in my milkshake,
You're with me in my favourite place,
You're the wind blowing in my face,
You're the Cha Cha to the slide,
You're like the glitter on my dress,
You're the smile on my face.

**Dawn Thomson (9)**
**High Blantyre Primary School, Glasgow**


# Mum

You're blue like a blueberry on a tree.
You're like the paint on my bedroom wall.
You're like the Lucozade going down into my tummy.
You're like pepperoni pizza covered in cheese.
You're like music in my ears.
You are the best mum I have ever known.

**Andrew Crombie (9)**
**High Blantyre Primary School, Glasgow**

# Mum

You're the sparkling shine of treasure.
You're my last bit of pleasure.
You're like my Uncle Eddie's boat.
You're like cheesy bits of pizza going down my throat.
You're like super comfy leather.
You're like a tickly little feather.
You're the sun rays going through the trees.
You're like buzzy little bees.
You're like the magic from Harry Potter.
You're the sun setting on the water.
Without you I wouldn't be here.
You're my mum and always will be.

**David Strain (9)**
**High Blantyre Primary School, Glasgow**


# Gordon's Dog Ben

On a nice day I go and play with my friend
His name is Gordon
He has blue eyes, blond hair and he is a fast runner!
He likes games and his dog Ben
Ben has white hair and little legs.
Ben barks very loud, *bark!*

**Andrew Roy (9)**
**High Blantyre Primary School, Glasgow**


# Miss Craig

When you get bullied in the playground
Miss Craig is always there with her black hood over her hair
And she'll help if you call
And if somebody pushes, she'll catch you before you fall.

**Hannah Geddes (9)**
**High Blantyre Primary School, Glasgow**

# My Mum

My mum is like a little star
She shines above me when it's dark.
My mum is like a cuddly bear
That cuddles me when I'm scared.
My mum is like a shiny sun,
That shines above me when it's dawn.
My mum is the best mum in the world,
She can do anything that makes me smile.

**Emma McLaughlan  (9)**
**High Blantyre Primary School, Glasgow**


# Uncle William

You're like a mirror in the sun.
You're like a star twinkling in the sky.
You're like an angel flying in the night.
You're like a pizza in the middle,
You're like a soft blue violet brightening up the dark sky,
You're like a footballer that's going to be a professional
But most of all you are my uncle William.

**William McBride  (9)**
**High Blantyre Primary School, Glasgow**


# Mum

You're like the colour violet on my skirt,
You're like the cheese hanging down the side of my pizza,
You're like the sunset in Florida that I could watch all day long.
You're like the music going into my ears,
I could play and play all day,
When I listen to the music a smile pops upon my face.
Mum, you're the bestest mum ever,
And when you touch me there's always a smile upon my face.

**Nicole Dick  (10)**
**High Blantyre Primary School, Glasgow**

# The Blue Balloon

My balloon is great.
I love my balloon.
I play with it all day.
I think it is good fun.
It only cost me five pence.

I got it before someone else got it.
It stretched so big, then went so small.
It was the best balloon I ever had in my life.

**Nicola Watson (7)**
**High Blantyre Primary School, Glasgow**


# My Cats

My cats can be funny.
My cats can be smart.
My cats can do something unusual.
My cats are fluffy.
My cats are cute.
My cats are my favourite cats in the world.

**Michael Reed (9)**
**High Blantyre Primary School, Glasgow**


# My Balloon

My balloon.
Got it in Troon,
Slipped out of my hand fast.
Well
Balloons never last!

**Colin Russell (8)**
**High Blantyre Primary School, Glasgow**

# My Purple Balloon

When I went to the balloon shop,
What did I see?
A lovely purple balloon staring at me.

Big, shiny purple
And it had a little face.

When I got it I was so happy.
Then it slipped out of my hand
And started to fly up into the sky.

What a rude thing to do
To go away without saying,

Goodbye.

**Emma Druggan  (8)**
**High Blantyre Primary School, Glasgow**


# My Best Friend

I have a best friend, his name is Ross.
He is a good friend but when he shouts you would not like him.
He is very good at skating,
He hardly ever falls.
Sometimes we fall out but in the end we fall back in.

**Conor Cooper  (9)**
**High Blantyre Primary School, Glasgow**


# Fear

Fear is as scary as a black tunnel
It tastes like out of date bread.
It smells like socks, as smelly as a skunk.
It looks like a graveyard.
It sounds like a rash with cars.
It feels like a ghost touching me.

**Jamie Low  (10)**
**Hills Trust Primary School, Glasgow**

# Calm/Despair

*Calm*
Peaceful village
Beautiful beach.
Children laughing
Sounds of people
Playing games
The beach was as calm as a sleeping kitten.
People were totally relaxed and happy.

*Despair*
Wasted buildings in a heap of rubble.
People crying in death and despair
People who are trapped screaming, 'Help!'
The land was as quiet and destroyed as a ghost town.
People were scared and frightened and wondering if they would live.

**Ross McMahon (11)**
**Hills Trust Primary School, Glasgow**


# Happiness/Despair

*Happiness*
Sunshine, happiness, joy and glee
Children out to play
People splashing in the sea
As calm as a summer's day.

*Despair*
Rainy clouds, thundery winds
And rubble everywhere
Even the people can't do anything
But just grieve as they stand and stare.

**Deborah Mulholland (11)**
**Hills Trust Primary School, Glasgow**

# Happiness

Happiness is big like an apple.
It feels like a hot drink and looks like the colour pink.
Pink like a sweet and pink like a flamingo.
It reminds me of the fairground and the beach.
Let bitterness of bleach be forgotten.
Happiness feels like a pillow that is soft.
It sounds like the sound of the sea and the hooting of a golden eagle.

**Rhoda McKechnie  (9)**
**Hills Trust Primary School, Glasgow**


# Hate

Hate is lonely, it makes you sad.
Hate is when you feel bad.
Hate is when you get mad.
Hate is when you want to hit out.
Hate is horrible and you shout.
Hate is when you dislike,
Hate is anger and when you fight.

**Calvin Borland  (9)**
**Hills Trust Primary School, Glasgow**


# Happiness

Happiness is yellow like the smiling sun
Happiness tastes like a creamy bun
Happiness smells like my mum
Happiness looks like juicy Hubba Bubba gum
Happiness sounds like a lovely hum
Happiness feels like the smoothness of a drum.

**Bobby Morrell  (9)**
**Hills Trust Primary School, Glasgow**

# Love

People love each other and they have fear.
But love is a powerful feeling in your heart.
It smells like perfume and it feels great.
When people are in love, they kiss and cuddle.
They give presents like roses, perfume and jewellery.
But then love can get powerful and you can get married.

**Lauren Gracey  (9)**
**Hills Trust Primary School, Glasgow**


# Hate

Hate is horror, hate is fear
Never hate, never say hate.
There is no such thing as hating kids because we are all mates.
Love is my faith; hate is not in our fate.
Be my mate, hate is out of date.
It's never too late to fight hate.

**Amin Fayaz  (10)**
**Hills Trust Primary School, Glasgow**


# Rain Is Like . . .

Rain is like water dripping from a big huge tap.
Rain is like little bits of snow flowing from the sky.
Rain is like rainbow drops falling from a rainbow,
Rain is like blue juice falling from the sky.

**Kimberly Ferguson  (9)**
**Hills Trust Primary School, Glasgow**


# Clouds Are Like . . .

Clouds are like sheep floating in the sky.
Rain is like silver ribbons floating from the sky.

**Chelsea Mills  (9)**
**Hills Trust Primary School, Glasgow**

# Snow Is Like . . .

Snow is like . . .
Sugar sprinkling from the pretty popcorn clouds and the
                              beautiful blue sky.
Snowdrops falling from the white puffy clouds and the gorgeous sky.
Cotton wool dripping from the sky and the golden clouds.

**Chelsea Geddes  (9)**
Hills Trust Primary School, Glasgow


# Earth Looks like . . .

Earth looks like a green and blue tennis ball spinning all around.
Earth sounds like the wind whistling and going round and round.
Earth feels like a circle going too fast.
Earth moves like a cheetah, running round and round.
Earth smells like the sea waving around.

**Michael McKechnie  (8)**
Hills Trust Primary School, Glasgow


# Snow Is Like . . .

Snow is like tulips falling from the sky,
Snow is like ice cream splashing on the wall,
Snow is like white butterflies dropping from the dull sky.

**Emma McLachlan  (8)**
Hills Trust Primary School, Glasgow


# Snow Is Like . . .

Snow is like sugar spilt on the floor.
Snow is like sunflowers bursting out of their buds.
Snow is like butterflies flying in the sky.

**Erin Armstrong  (8)**
Hills Trust Primary School, Glasgow

# Calm/Despair

*Calm*
Peaceful village
Beautiful scenery
Sea splashing
Excited people
Feeling happy and relaxed.

*Despair*
People hurt
Sick people
Running away
People crying
Footsteps
Car alarms.

**Christopher Mills  (11)**
Hills Trust Primary School, Glasgow

# A Puzzle Poem

I am small,
I am yellow
When I am a baby
I can fly
What am I?

A: Ladybird.

**Luke Burring  (7)**
Hills Trust Primary School, Glasgow

# Puzzle Poem

I am brown and slimy
I have a hard shell
I leave a trail
What am I?

A: Snail.

**Dylan Kerr  (7)**
Hills Trust Primary School, Glasgow

# A Puzzle Poem

I live in the sea
I'm like a star
I've got little bumps on me.
What am I?

A: Starfish.

**Derek Bowden  (6) & Matthew MacGregor  (7)**
Hills Trust Primary School, Glasgow


# A Puzzle Poem

I am black and hairy
Some people like me, some do not.
What am I?

A: Spider.

**Muskan Saigal  (6) & Lauren McCormick  (7)**
Hills Trust Primary School, Glasgow


# A Puzzle Poem

I have got wings and they are colourful.
My wings have the same colours on each side.
What am I?

A: Butterfly.

**Anna Tinarwo  (6)**
Hills Trust Primary School, Glasgow


# A Puzzle Poem

I am red with black spots
I live on a leaf
What am I?

A: Ladybird.

**Abdikarim Adan  (7)**
Hills Trust Primary School, Glasgow

# Fear

Fear is like a ghost who will not leave you alone.
He follows you everywhere you go.
You try to tell your parents but they don't understand.
You tell them you are having nightmares so that you can sleep
with them.
Your mum finally takes you on holiday to take your mind off it,
But he comes with you.
You wish it could just go away.
You hate whoever invented fear.

Fear tastes like a jug of out of date milk.
It smells like dung.
It looks like the black hole of Calcutta.

Hallowe'en comes, you are so scared,
You don't want to go out dressed up like everyone else,
But your mum insists.
So you go as a pumpkin.
You see a witch; you are so scared you run away.

**Beccy Webster  (9)**
**Hills Trust Primary School, Glasgow**

# Calm/Despair

*Calm*
The scene was beautiful and the sounds of people were like
a calm sea.
People were very relaxed and happy and the beach was as calm
as a sleeping cat.

*Despair*
The scene was a disaster because of all the ruined homes.
There was crying babies, petrified people, frightened babies
People trapped and drying.

**Sean McManus  (11)**
**Hills Trust Primary School, Glasgow**

# Hope/Despair

*Hope*
Calm sea like a soft duvet.
People talking like the air whispering.
Speed boats like the wind blowing on trees.

*Despair*
Car alarms going off like someone breaking into a warehouse.
Babies crying like seagulls trying to get a fish.
People screaming as if they were at a rock concert.

**Connie Douglas  (11)**
Hills Trust Primary School, Glasgow

# Love

Love is like a big red heart.
It tastes like sweets.
It smells like a big garden.
It sounds like wind and a breeze.
It feels like smooth grass.

**Tyla Young  (10)**
Hills Trust Primary School, Glasgow

# A Puzzle Poem

I have got black and yellow stripes
I love honey
I fly all about the garden.
What am I?

A: Bee.

**Jacob Duncan Atkinson  (7)**
Hills Trust Primary School, Glasgow

# The Four Seasons

First there comes the patterned leaves
Dancing and prancing through the trees.
So smooth and bouncy, there must be a reason,
This is the start of the four seasons.
Spring comes first,
With its leaves soft and green.
Where they group up like a football team.
Then comes summer, they're floating still,
The beaming yellow sun.
That's when I'll go to Menora - I'll run.
Then there comes autumn,
With a lively breeze.
With the red, yellow and orange prancing leaves.
The crispy broken branches blowing without its green.
And last but not least, winter,
With its fluffy, bouncy, white snow,
It glistens in my eyes and that's how I know.
This is the end of my short little poem.

**Erin Armstrong  (9)**
**Houston Primary School, Houston**


# Living In Transylvania

If you live in Transylvania
And you're in your house one night,
Then there's a knocking on your door
That wakes you with a fright.
And you rush downstairs
And standing there
Is a figure pale and green,
If he says he is Count Dracula
Just pray it's Hallowe'en!

**Duncan Webb  (9)**
**Houston Primary School, Houston**

# At The School Prom

Young glamorous children were dancing with pride
And all were standing side by side
The music was booming off every wall
It seemed to echo off the silver ball
The gym hall was overflowing
And seemed to keep on going
The stage was glittering, glamorous and glimmering
And every one was sitting
The table was shining and sparkling bright
I ended up doing the dance of the night
Right outside guided by the moonlight
The pupils went way outside
To take a last look at the best time of life
Which was the one, the only
*The massive blue school!*
They were leaving behind.

**Kelly McGarvey (9)**
**Houston Primary School, Houston**


# Head-Head-Head-Headbang

As Slipknot headbang on the stage,
The riot turns into a rage.
'Head!-Head!-Head!-Headbang' comes the cry,
And the riot begins to fry.
A drunken lout staggers out,
Then gets dragged back into the violent pit
And gets his last glimpse of the freaky masks as his head is hit.
Bottles are smashed,
The stage is trashed,
And the survivors start limping home.

**Michael Love (9)**
**Houston Primary School, Houston**

# The Terrifying Monster

I woke up needing water
Then I heard a thump
The vibration shook the milk
And it fell on my head with a bump.
I felt my head and it had a lump
I went outside and the first thing I saw was its dirty toenails,
Its slimy skin made me jump
Its shiny red eyes looking at me
Its pointy horns made me shiver
Its endless tail had scales on it
And worst of all were its rotten teeth.

Then it turned round,
I looked at its back and it had a bleeping thing
I pulled it out and the monster made a loud sound,
It coughed out a pop singer and a doorbell ringer,
Then it turned round again and smiled at me cheerfully.

**Mark Yuill (9)**
**Houston Primary School, Houston**


# Home Sweet Home

It was home sweet home that brightened my days,
The TV flashing,
But still I couldn't put my homework astray,
The motionless polished table glancing at me,
My tasty dinner tasting as it's supposed to be,
The beautiful pictures lay quiet on the wall,
As the clock ticked to nine o'clock,
Last but not least my bed keeps me warm,
As long as I can snuggle while the covers are on,
All these come from home . . . sweet . . . home.

**Beth Haughan (9)**
**Houston Primary School, Houston**

# My Pets

My pets are rabbits,
Bigwig and Hazel are their names,
They have a big hutch,
We built it ourselves,
They live outside; spring, autumn, summer and winter,
Their cover flaps in the night,
It sometimes gives me a fright,
When the weather is cold the water freezes,
The noises and wind teases them when their cover is down,
The food is grainy and spills a lot,
The plank is wet when it rains,
And it's soggy too,
They get out when it's dry,
And love the sky blue.

**Katie McCowan (9)**
**Houston Primary School, Houston**


# My Game Boy

I am really pleased with my brand new toy
My silver fancy Game Boy
I have now become a really big fan
Of a tricky game called Rayman
I press the buttons till my fingers ache
Then my mum shouts out, 'Put it away for goodness sake!'
Jumping on rocks, swinging on trees
Fighting the baddies till they're down on their knees
I keep playing it more and more
Trying to get the highest score
It's been really fun but I have to go
I think my batteries are running low.

**Rebecca Greenaway (9)**
**Houston Primary School, Houston**

# Football

The teams walk out of the tunnel,
Fans scream as loud as funnels,
The teams to their goals,
There's no holes in the pitch
Celtic in their green and white strip,
Rangers in royal blue kit,
And the game's off.
Rangers with the ball . . . *goal!*
One-nil,
The shot was hard but standing still are
The goals,
Two minutes to go,
It's two-nil.
That's the thrill,
The fans go home happy.

**Michael Bonner  (9)**
Houston Primary School, Houston


# Football

On the big green pitch,
That was cut perfectly,
A round smooth ball,
Was moving so smoothly,
I caught sight of players,
Doing fancy tricks,
The excited crowd,
Shouting their team on,
There's the bossy referee,
Blowing his loud whistle,
Then I saw white posts,
Glistening in the sun,
Oh no,
The other team scored which made it one-one.

**Cameron Brown  (9)**
Houston Primary School, Houston

# Dream Night

Lying in my cosy bed,
Silent and deep in sleeping
But inside my busy head
I am really dreaming.
And under my duvet,
So warm and puffy,
Making me feel,
So hot and stuffy.
Then all of a sudden
I feel myself,
Being lifted from my
Sleeping rest!
And now I feel myself
Under the sea
With the glistening, salty sea.
All around me.
All the disturbed water,
Turning into each wave,
Then appearing in front of me,
A huge stone cave.
And the whirling waves
Slapping on its sides,
I've never seen such a cave,
As the water glides.
Oh and then a whipping whirlpool
Swirling round and round
Then all of a sudden,
I feel my feet on the ground.
And here I am in my bed
But there's still more dreams in my head.

**Katie McKinlay (9)**
**Houston Primary School, Houston**

# The Aeroplane

Flying high,
In the sky,
The people in the aeroplane,
Watching the telly,
In front of cramped chairs on which they sat,
They had their trays out flat,
As the wings soared through the air,
The round wheels were tucked in the floor,
You could not get to them through the door,
The shiny windows on the walls,
Were half closed with their shades,
Remember the people watching telly,
They saw the poor man inside fall on his belly,
But you can't forget the captain,
With his big top hat,
If it wasn't for him
They wouldn't let the people in.

**Louise Calderwood  (9)**
**Houston Primary School, Houston**


# The Rainbow

Once I saw a lovely colourful, shimmering rainbow,
That glistened and gleamed with its seven colours
In one big bright arch.
The seven colours are:
Red, the colour of fire,
Orange, the colour of carrots,
Blue, the colour of the sea,
Yellow, the colour of the sun,
Green, the colour of grass,
Pink, the colour of a heart,
And violet, the last colour of the rainbow.
The colour of a crocus.

**Hannah Thomson  (9)**
**Houston Primary School, Houston**

# The Football Match

I was sitting in a seat at Old Trafford down in England,
I watched the brilliant players sprint,
I couldn't miss the rusty old goals that were just standing,
I watched the good manager shouting
At his players, 'You over there, where you're supposed to be?'
I saw the referee, though I didn't think he was very good,
But I'm sure he was in a good mood,
He blew his whistle with such pride,
Then I heard the angry supporters,
Shouting at the referee,
It's a free kick on the bright green grass,
Which was cut perfectly with
Lines up and down the park,
It was near the end of the game
When the player shoots with the
Golden boot,
The ball flies through the air,
It smacks the back of the net,
And it's a *goal!*

**Ruairidh Fitzpatrick  (9)**
**Houston Primary School, Houston**


# The Funfair

The sweet pink candyfloss is melting in my mouth
The teacups spinning round and round
Make me feel quite dizzy
Then the big wheel
Can't forget about that
It's going really slow, not as fast as a bat
The colourful stalls are being played
By loads of people
The giant roller coaster is bobbing up and down.

**Hannah Corr  (9)**
**Houston Primary School, Houston**

# The Nightmare

The monsters, the monsters
On the roof, enveloped by darkness
Then boom! Nameless creatures thumping on the roof
Wait! What's that looming towards me?
Is it Mum?
No!
It's a zombie!
A rasping zombie that is moaning.
The gradually breaking bed, standing still
And then the bloodcurdling cry that pierced the air.
It's too freaky
That cemetery.
Creeping horror of the cemetery coming through the night.
Staring through the night.
I hear a voice.
'We're coming to get you!'
No! It's too much!
'Hush! Dear, it's only a dream!'

**Josh Penman  (9)**
**Houston Primary School, Houston**


# My Dad

My dad embarrasses me at boring old school
Because he runs to give me a kiss
Before the bell goes.
He knocks over smelly dustbins
And runs away as fast as he can go.
He puts the sound up on the television until it blares
But watches the clock over there.
He pretends he's a musician and plays my recorder
My greedy dad eats a huge breakfast
But he is the best dad in the world
And he couldn't get any better.

**Erin Murray  (9)**
**Houston Primary School, Houston**

# School So Long Ago

It was so long ago but I see it today,
The doors lying open.
I remember the teacher calling us in from playtime.
So long ago.
The windows lying open and smashed.
I remember the way they seemed to sparkle.
So long ago.
I noticed the walls lying in wrecks.
I remember the nice colour that was covered on them.
So long ago.
I looked down to the playground.
The games still on the ground.
Being destroyed by the weather.
I remember playing hopscotch with my friends.
So long ago.
I went down the hill.
I looked through a window I saw my classroom.
I remember the teacher talking to the other teachers.
So long ago.
I noticed the computers standing on their stand.
All broken and not turned on.
I remember the computer lessons I was good at.
So long ago.
And that's all I remember now.
For now I'm sixty-two.

**Stephen Hedges (10)**
**Houston Primary School, Houston**


# Football

The football, as hard as a brick,
Was getting kicked
The giant stadium with lots of people in it
And I wished the bossy ref would fall in a pit.
The excited fans cheering on the great team
As the broad goal nets were getting blown like a stream.

**Andrew Campbell (9)**
**Houston Primary School, Houston**

# The Snow

Staring out the window
Watching the snowflakes
They twinkle as they tumble
Down to the ground
They make no sound
As they fall down and down
Making the sheet of snow thicker and thicker
When the snowflakes fall quicker and quicker
Dogs inside, far too hot
They can't even move a jot
It's too cold for a walk
The cold air means we can't talk
Well I'm watching TV
It's far too cold for me
I'm watching and watching the TV
When I call to my mum
'Hot chocolate for me,'
I drink my hot chocolate, yummy, yum, yum
I look out the window
As I call to my mum,
'Come, come
The snow's gone off.
Can I go out and build a snowman and have a shout?'

**Kirsten Robertson  (8)**
Houston Primary School, Houston


# My Cat's Belongings

Her very colourful basket,
Is covered in black and white hair,
The soft brush strokes her fur,
Her fun toys are rolling on the floor,
The smelly food is waiting to be gobbled,
Her white litter tray is getting emptied,
The very clean water is lying in her bowl.

**Beth Gormley  (9)**
Houston Primary School, Houston

# The Stables

As I approached the stables,
I heard the horses neigh.
I said to myself,
'I'm here wahey!'
As I went to muck out one of the smelly stables,
I found a raw carrot on one of the tables.
So I gave it to a horse,
She snorted thankfully.
As she licked my hand,
I giggled with glee.
My teacher was putting hay into a net.
I have to give it to my pony,
How could I forget!
As the horses cantered,
It made the riding school start thumping.
I heard the tapping of the crops,
And the horses' hooves clumping.
I saw the ponies galloping in the fields far away.
Horses always run about,
If it is a sunny day!
When I come to the stables,
I feel over the moon,
Goodbye, I'd better go!
My riding class starts soon!

**Laura McNeill (9)**
**Houston Primary School, Houston**


# The Church Clock

When I was in Paisley
I heard the church clock chime
I looked, it told me the time
It was six o'clock
I remembered at six o'clock I had to meet my mum
So I headed down to the shiny wooden dock,
And there was my mum in her bright pink frock.

**Grant Cadden (9)**
**Houston Primary School, Houston**

# The Devil

David takes a trip to meet the Devil.
He lands in a black rock-boat,
With one of the Devil's goats.
Not an ordinary goat,
It is steering the black rock-boat.
It is made of rocks,
'Help,' cried David, 'help, help, help!'
'I'm in a rock-boat steered by a rock-goat,
Why am I not sinking?
I'm in a lava river!'
Boiling lava spotted with black rock-boats,
Of course all steered by a black rock-goat.
On he went seeing slaves being whipped with orange fire ships.
He saw giant fire monsters,
At least forty-feet high.
Soldiers of the Devil, all big, fierce and boiling hot.
The field of fire came into view - can never be put out,
And alas, he sees Fire Mountain,
The home of the Devil.
Spitting lava, a stream flowing down the side.
He jumps out of the black rock-boat, steered by the black rock-goat.
In the fifty-feet high, door all made of rock.
He sees the Devil, Sir Ironsoul at his side.
The Devil holding a triple-bladed trident,
Has horns and is a human of fire.
The Devil cried, 'David,' Sir Ironsoul moved towards David
His sword missed, inches from David's throat.

**Struan Grant  (9)**
**Houston Primary School, Houston**

# The Lollipop

There was the old sweet shop standing all alone,
I ran into the glorious sweet shop as quickly as I could,
As I ran my money shone and jingled when it sat in my pocket,
The lollipop sat in a plastic box and it was gleaming and it
looked wonderful,
I grabbed the soft cardboard stick that joined on to the
glorious lollipop,
The plastic crinkled wrapper went round the sweet I bought
the lollipop,
A super lovely smell came off the lolly as I sucked it all the
way home.

**Tomas Canning  (9)**
**Houston Primary School, Houston**


# My Rabbit

I went out to my garden
My dad said, 'What are you looking for Scott?'
I replied, 'I'm looking for Poppet'
Then my mum came out wearing a frock
I looked away and saw the food
The straw was still and golden
I couldn't miss the bitten cover, very holey indeed
The water was glistening in the sun
I noticed the wooden posts and Poppet peeked out.

**Scott Murphy  (9)**
**Houston Primary School, Houston**


# Snowflake

Slipping, twirling, twisting, fluttering,
Swaying, drifting, floating,
Tumbling, wandering, cartwheeling,
Quickly.
Gliding and circling quietly.

**Anna Weaver-Sharpe  (9)**
**Killermont Primary School, Bearsden**

# This New Girl In My Class

This new girl in my class,
She looks polite and neat,
But you would never notice that,
She was a right wee *cheek!*

This new girl in my class,
She looks polite and neat,
But you would never notice that,
She was *never* sweet!

**Clara Mitchell (8)**
**Killermont Primary School, Bearsden**


# Tsunami, The Disaster

I am the tsunami! I am the tsunami!
Washing, killing, drowning, crashing.
I am the tsunami! I am the tsunami!
Fast and big,
Crushing and floating,
Killing everybody in my way.

**Kenneth Vickers (9)**
**Killermont Primary School, Bearsden**


# Plague

I am the plague! I am the plague!
Swarming! Scourging! Invading! Attacking!
I am the plague! I am the plague!
Infecting and deadly,
Contagious and deathly.
I infect all in my path.

**Peter Thorpe (9)**
**Killermont Primary School, Bearsden**

# Football

Kicking, running, shooting, scoring,
Pushing, hacking, fouling,
Sliding, shoulder barging, dribbling, pulling,
Going off, going on, winning!

**Yi Fei Yang (9)**
**Killermont Primary School, Bearsden**


# My Dog Zack

Rolling, playing, slavering, swimming
Running, eating, retrieving.
Shaking, drinking, romping, panting
Chewing, scrounging, barking.

**Harley Smith (9)**
**Killermont Primary School, Bearsden**


# Snowflake

Circling, plopping. Flying, swirling,
Cart wheeling, gliding, meandering,
Diving, flying, rolling, twirling,
Whirling, floating, wandering.

**Beth Trodden (9)**
**Killermont Primary School, Bearsden**


# Tornado

Violent, wild, windy, raging,
Murderous, gusty, forceful,
Turbulent, stormy, rough, rampaging,
Devastating, blustery, powerful.

**Robbie Pollock (9)**
**Killermont Primary School, Bearsden**

# Flood

I am the flood!
I am the flood!
Sinking! Rippling! Soaking! Swamping!
I am the flood!
I am the flood!
Splashing and sploshing,
Wet and washing,
I soak all in my way.

**Colin Malaney (9)**
**Killermont Primary School, Bearsden**


# Whirlwind

I am the whirlwind!
I am the whirlwind!
Roaring! Whistling! Blowing! Swirling!
I am the whirlwind!
I am the whirlwind!
Fast and furious,
Quick and curious,
I pick up rubbish in my way.

**Josh Sorbie (9)**
**Killermont Primary School, Bearsden**


# Fear

Fear is scarlet.
Fear smells like pain.
Fear tastes like rotten eggs.
Fear sounds like war.
Fear feels scary and hard.
Fear lives deep, dark in a pitch-black cave.

**Farah Sadiq (9)**
**Killermont Primary School, Bearsden**

# Poverty

Poverty is pain, disease and death.
It smells like smoke, fire and coal.
Poverty tastes mouldy, old and stale.
It sounds like an echo going through a cave.
It feels bitter, cold and rough.
Poverty lives in the heart of a sin.

**Lucy Liveston (9)**
**Killermont Primary School, Bearsden**


# The Fire Of London

I am the fire! I am the fire!
Spreading, scorching, roaring and rumbling!
Deafening, clashing, crashing and tumbling!
Flushing, roasting, frying and burning!
Cooking, crackling, fizzing and churning!

**Sam McLean (9)**
**Killermont Primary School, Bearsden**


# Hallowe'en

Dark, weird, thunderstorm, scary,
Dress-up, grave, night.
Bats, purple, pumpkin, hairy,
Orange, black, fright!

**Daniel Keller (9)**
**Killermont Primary School, Bearsden**


# Football

Kicking, nicking, cheering, hearing,
Heading, defending, hoping,
Joking, scoring, roaring, scoring,
Thrashing, bashing, clashing.

**Grant Halley (9)**
**Killermont Primary School, Bearsden**

# Disaster Strikes!

I am the volcano!
I am the volcano!
Melting, sizzling, slithering, creeping.
I am the volcano!
I am the volcano!
Burning and leaping,
Calling and screaming,
I will melt everything in my way!

**Fiona Mackenzie (9)**
**Killermont Primary School, Bearsden**


# Loneliness

Loneliness is a dull grey,
It smells like mould and teabags.
Loneliness tastes like raw vegetables,
It sounds silent and chilly.
Loneliness feels cold and icy.
Loneliness lives on the cold banks of a motionless river . . .

**Karen Heaney (9)**
**Killermont Primary School, Bearsden**


# Tsunami

I am the tsunami! I am the tsunami!
Giant! Curling! Devastating! Crashing!
I am the tsunami! I am the tsunami!
Powerful and dashing,
Spinning and crashing,
Destroying everything in my path.

**Jack Byrne (9)**
**Killermont Primary School, Bearsden**

# Bin

Outside in the rain,
Wet and slimy,
Cold and shivery,
Stands the bin.

Outside in the sun,
Warm and snug,
Cosy and smiley,
Stands the bin!

**Jessica Greenhalgh  (9)**
**Killermont Primary School, Bearsden**


# Earthquake

I am the earthquake! I am the earthquake!
Rumbling! Roaring! Destroying! Crushing!
I am the earthquake! I am the earthquake!
Quick and furious,
Fierce and curious,
I will destroy everything in my way.

**Sarah Hooper  (9)**
**Killermont Primary School, Bearsden**


# Tsunami Disaster

I'm the tsunami! I'm the tsunami!
Crushing! Killing! Drowning! And sweeping away!
I'm the tsunami! I'm the tsunami!
Until you're out of breath!
Run, run, then you'll meet your death!

**Maighdlin Gold  (9)**
**Killermont Primary School, Bearsden**

# Music

It starts off as a word or note
And then becomes a lyric
Then it's like buttons on a coat
And that's the start of music.
Now instruments they must be cool
Like a rock guitar or drums
And in music there are no rules
Famous, here we come!
Let's make the tickets for our gig
For £4.28
If you sell enough you'll be big
And maybe even great.
Go and enter the big, bad stage
The crowd are all huge fans
Remember, music has its rage
And that's how you make a band!

**Eric Corson  (9)**
**Killermont Primary School, Bearsden**


# Competition

C ompetition, please let me win
O r at least tell why this poem's a sin
M um and Dad wished me luck
P oppy my cousin said I should win
E nd this poem now and I bet I win
T his isn't a joke!
I 'll say this time I'll let you off
T hen one day I'm sure to buff
I want to win this, really I do
O n this fine day, my only chance
N o way am I going to lose!

**Rachael Horne  (9)**
**Killermont Primary School, Bearsden**

# I Saw It!

I was in my fishing boat
Fishing for pike
Then I saw it
Swimming in the sea.
Was it a shark?
A golden pike
Or maybe my next door neighbour Mike?

I cast my rod out
Really far
I think I got it!
*What is it?*
I said to myself.
The golden pike
Came out of the water.
I cried, 'My Lord!
I got a whopper!'
The pike opened its mouth.
'You're a naughty little tyke!'

I left the bay
Then vowed that
I'll be back another day!

**Connor Galbraith (9)**
**Killermont Primary School, Bearsden**


# Best Friends

A friend is kind,
Sharing.
A friend is generous,
Caring.

A friend is nice,
Cheerful.
A friend is honest,
Grateful.

**Eilidh Grant (9)**
**Killermont Primary School, Bearsden**

# Smack Down Vs Raw

Kicking, punching, climbing, slapping,
Grabbing, jumping, choking,
Running, throwing, stamping, whacking,
Lying, kneeling, poking.

**Fraser Eide (9)**
**Killermont Primary School, Bearsden**


# My Dad

My dad is very funny
He acts like a clown
He always talks me into things
Like spending time on the beach
He's always on the phone
And tells me to be quiet
Sometimes he is sad
When I don't give him a cuddle
But let's not talk about that now
His favourite hobby is plane spotting
He likes to drink tea
He hates to drink coffee
His favourite thing to eat is a scone
He's very nice and friendly
But there's one thing I hate
He laughs whenever I'm hurt
He loves ginger cats
He's a very exciting dad
He helps me with my homework
Believe me, he is the best dad.

**Susannah Wallwork (8)**
**Langbank Primary School, Langbank**

# Through That Door

Through that door
Is ancient Egypt
With people walking on the sand
And people building pyramids
By the river Nile

Through that door
Is a sweety land
With chocolate,
Gummy Bears
And gingerbread men

Through that door
Is back home
And this is
The end of my poem.

**Beth Irwin  (7)**
**Langbank Primary School, Langbank**


# A Portrait Of Winter

Dark days and dark nights,
Thundering storms that give me a fright.

Snow falls hard, as hard as can be,
Outside stands a Christmas tree.

Stockings hang upon the wall,
Mistletoe in the hall.

Tonight's when he comes,
Jolly Saint Nick, our fat, old chum.

I run downstairs and what do I see?
The glorious presents he left for me!

I can't wait till next year, it's so much fun,
But maybe sometimes I'd like some sun.

**Kathryn Lapping  (9)**
**Langbank Primary School, Langbank**

# A Portrait Of Winter

The snow and the fire
The hats and the scarves
The snowmen and hailstones
Make winter, it's all part

By the warm fire
Out of the snow
The snowmen play with their hats and coats
The icicles wobble with a shiny gleam
They make winter, it's all part

The snowball fights
Children laughing
Your family together
Everyone's happy
All make winter
And all an important part

The tasty food
The delicious treats
You're happy enjoying yourself
You wish it would never be over
Hopefully your wish will come true.

**Gemma McKenzie (9)**
**Langbank Primary School, Langbank**


# My Daddy

As strong as a house
As funny as a circus clown
As fun as a puppy
As clever as a cat
As loving as an angel
As handsome as a prince
He's fab, just like me!

**David Small (8)**
**Langbank Primary School, Langbank**

# A Portrait Of Winter

Winter is my favourite season
The snow is really great
And I always build a snowman
With my best mate

I wrap up warm
Go sledging a lot
And when I get home
I have something hot

The snow is falling
The rain has gone
After all that
You might yawn

I have snowball fights
Never win
But winter's still
A great thing!

**Jennifer Mackay (9)**
**Langbank Primary School, Langbank**


# Through That Door

Through that door
There is a future city
Hovercrafts flying
And lots of new fashions to wear
There is always something going on

Through that door
Is ancient Egyptian life
Lot of slaves building pyramids
Many people working on buildings by the Nile
Guards giving orders
Watch out!
They are coming your way!

**Blair Billings (8)**
**Langbank Primary School, Langbank**

# The Surprise

Waiting, waiting, waiting
For the dolphin fun to begin
Waiting, waiting, waiting
For the signal to swim
Waiting, waiting, waiting
For the splashing of the fin
And to hear the dolphins sing
Time to eat, time to play
Time to swim with a ray
Hold on tightly to the dolphin's fin
It is now time for you to swim
Each dolphin is different
No two are the same
Each likes to play its own favourite game
Red, yellow, pink and blue
Fish swim by in every hue
Waiting, waiting, waiting
For our place in the queue
Was there ever such waiting,
Such waiting before?

**Andrew Galt  (11)**
**Langbank Primary School, Langbank**


# In The Winter

In the winter I love the snow
When you're on the sledge it will go
In the winter there's a lot of rain
But you can't allow it to be a pain

In the winter the hills are white
Which makes the world look really bright
In the winter there's not much sun
But you can still have lots of fun.

**Kyle Rafferty  (9)**
**Langbank Primary School, Langbank**

# In My Mind

My mind is one of a kind,
In it you will find,
The horrors of the underworld,
Creeping up your spine,
Scary monsters, vampire bats,
Terrible black, biting cats,
That is what you will find,
In my mind.

In my mind,
I've climbed to the highest,
And have flown like a bird,
I know this sounds ridiculous,
It really sounds absurd,
I've walked two hundred miles,
I've kept pet crocodiles,
That is what you will find,
In my mind.

In my mind,
Are rugby players,
Playing as rough as big, brown bears,
Scrumming and line outs,
People betting, having doubts,
In my mind are Dad and Mum,
I love them both very much,
I hope they love me too,
Love me as their son and more,
That is what you will find,
In my mind.

**Cameron Gilchrist (9)**
**Langbank Primary School, Langbank**

# What Is Through That Door?

Through that door there are sweeties galore!
From tiny gumdrops to massive Allsorts,
There's everything here so you'll never be bored
With all the wonderful tastes.
Giant gingerbread men come to life
And dance 'round with candy canes.
Whenever you're hungry you know where to go,
Just simply walk through that door.

Through that door is a city of our future
1000 years ahead of us
Just waiting to be explored.
From its giant spacecraft to its lifelike holograms,
Even a theme park way up on the moon.
Millions of other inventions,
You'd think you're having a dream!
If you ever want fun you know where to go,
Just simply walk through that door.

**Ben Saunders (9)**
**Langbank Primary School, Langbank**


# The Snyke

The Snyke is a cunning beast
Who likes to feast
On rats and mice
And everything that is not nice.

He sleeps in a burrow far underground
His snores are a terrible sound
All the other creatures keep away
The smell, the sound could ruin their day.

Like a fox and a hare the Snyke is very fast
Blink and he's past
Nobody likes the Snyke
Because they think he is a mischievous tyke.

**Jennifer Gilchrist (11)**
**Langbank Primary School, Langbank**

# In My Bed!

I hear the rain battering off my window,
And the wind spitting against my house,
People chatting through the night,
And the owl howling with a fright!
I hear my mum and dad's TV on,
I see shadows creeping around my room,
And flashes of light beaming from the other rooms,
The stars settling in the sky,
And the moon shining on the calm Clyde.
I smell the fresh toast,
And the flowers from downstairs.
The sweet tea from the other room,
I feel warm in my cosy bed,
And happy I have got a bed,
So I can have a good night's sleep tonight!

**James McGuinness  (11)**
**Langbank Primary School, Langbank**


# My Papa

My papa used to smell of newspapers
His hair was white and grey
I used to like to play with it and put it up with a bobble
His eyes were blue and twinkled when I looked at him
He had a smile on his wrinkly face
He used to say, 'Come on, let's play.'
He'd sit on his chair reading his newspaper
He'd help in the kitchen making lots of food
He had a kind of soft voice, he hardly talked
He wore a jumper and tie
He was very ill and he never said.
My papa was the best.

**Natalie Hakeem  (9)**
**Langbank Primary School, Langbank**

# My Brother

My brother is very funny,
He's good at winding us up.
He can rap and dance like Eminem,
Though at times he tells me to shut up!
He keeps me safe and helps me do stuff
But when we're playing he's far too rough!

He's as handsome as Prince Charming,
Apart from when he's just out of bed!
He's as cheeky as a monkey
And as bossy as a bee
And although he's always loving
He *never* says he loves me!

He has brown, spiky hair
And gleaming, blue eyes.
He's as tall as my nana
And as strong as my dad!

He loves to play football
And likes to wear baggy clothes
But when he's in a bad mood
He wears a T-shirt and shorts
And, believe me, that isn't like him!
There may be some bad bits about him
But I still love him!

**Kate Abernethy  (8)**
**Langbank Primary School, Langbank**

# Egypt

E gyptians ruled the country
G reat mummies in the tombs
Y oung boys and girls born rich or poor
P haraohs bossing all the slaves
T he great river Nile slices the country.

**Daniel MacRae  (10)**
**Langbank Primary School, Langbank**

# Through That Door

Through that door is a jungle
Waiting for you to explore.
There are some alligators in the lake
Waiting for some fish.
Some monkeys are play with each other
Having fun.
In a hut a poacher is making his evil plans
To take over the jungle.
Some elephants are having baths.
I wonder what else there will be?
Some deer are getting chased,
Run away! Run away!
Here comes a helicopter.

Through the door is a haunted kingdom,
Big, black and gloomy.
When you step inside
You find a big suit of armour
With a feather coming out the top.
In the dining room it's dark and gloomy.
There's a big chunk of wood for the fire.
In the garden there are bones of the guard dog
And the only sound is the rain.

**Kate Sandeman (8)**
**Langbank Primary School, Langbank**


# A Motorway

Cars raging, traffic jam gaining, drivers shouting.
Christmas shoppers, flashing headlights.
Trucks taking time, taking up all the road.
The motorway is an erupting volcano.
Scorching exhausts, exploding horns.
Oil acting as volcanic acid, belches of acceleration.
Dormant at night but berserk in the morning.

**Matthew Ellis Evans (9)**
**Langbank Primary School, Langbank**

# School

The head teacher overflows with fiery smoke,
Then for a while she lies dormant,
Waiting to erupt.
In the playground the bullies wait to explode,
Their faces turn red.
The bell rings and everyone comes out.
The bullies soar across the playground,
Causing havoc everywhere,
The head teacher awakes, there is destruction everywhere.
The home time bell rings, the children leave,
They go home,
To leave their school extinct for a day,
Until they go back to commence the explosions and uproar,
For yet another day.

**Hamish McGowan  (9)**
**Langbank Primary School, Langbank**


# What If?

What if there was an Earth with no pollution?
What if every chair was a soft as a cushion?
What is there was no such thing as death?
What if nobody ever ran out of breath?

What if there was no such thing as greed?
What if everybody did a good deed?
What if nobody went to bed?
What if everybody stayed up instead?

What if everybody had a priceless bead?
What if everybody could succeed?
What if I could see lava being swirled?
What if we had a perfect world?

**Ryan Sweeney  (10)**
**Langbank Primary School, Langbank**

# The Snyke

The Snyke is slimy, green and gold,
Its snykeskin coat is bright and bold,
It has seven legs, long and straight,
A gigantic blue whale it hasn't yet ate,
Three black eyes on its head,
Boulders on the beach are its bed,
Four sharp ears it has on its face,
Shaped like a triangle, feels like lace,
Two large wings on its back,
Holding anything like a sack,
A big, long tail, spiked and green,
The little, red spot that can't be seen.
It eats up children for its tea,
I hope it doesn't eat up me,
With its big, sharp teeth - *crunch! Crunch!*
It's going to eat me for its lunch!
Run! Run! Down the lane,
This Snyke really is a pain,
It hope it's not going to eat me up,
It will drink my blood in a cup!
Into my house and up the stairs,
I'm safe now, who cares?

**Victoria Smith  (11)**
**Langbank Primary School, Langbank**

# Through The Door

In a crumbling, tumbling castle
Which towers over a dark, spooky forest
Inside the castle are dark steps
And up the steps is a door
And on the handle there is a note
It says, *Open If You Dare!*
Through the door are zombies and lots of secret trapdoors
There are tall, sharp axes
Gripped in their hands to hurt you.

**Errin Ann Roy  (7)**
**Langbank Primary School, Langbank**

# If I Were An Animal . . .

If I were an animal
A monkey I would be
Swinging freely
From tree to tree.

The feeling of the freedom
As if I were a queen
Beautiful sights
Everywhere to be seen.

I'd chatter with my family
And my monkey friends
From the minute the sun rises
Until the fun day ends.

So a monkey is the animal
That I would choose to be
Though I really must admit
I prefer to be me!

**Jennifer Burns  (10)**
**Langbank Primary School, Langbank**


# Through That Door

Through that door
Is the land of the kings
With slaves feeding the pharaoh grapes
The pyramids standing huge and tall
There is a mummifying procession taking place.

Through that door
Is a land of sweets
With gingerbread houses
Candyfloss pillows and candy cane lamp posts.

**Sam Ellis  (7)**
**Langbank Primary School, Langbank**

# Cold Christmas

It's winter and cold
Snowmen are made
Trees are bare
Snowball fights
Children are cold
The crackling fire
The children are warm now
But still wet
Snowmen outside
Now melt in the wind
The whistling wind
Sounds like moans
In the snow
The snow is soft
When you go outside
It's cold and wet
When you fall
Children are happy
In the snow.

**Alexander McCoist  (10)**
**Langbank Primary School, Langbank**


# Through That Door

Through that door
Is a magical treasure island
Where there are pirates
As bad as bad can be
Dragons look down for the nasty pirates
They are looking for pots of gold
Searching in dark, creepy caves
Using old, crumpled maps
The dragons begin to feel hungry
They're having pirates for tea!

**Jack Bell  (7)**
**Langbank Primary School, Langbank**

# My Dad

My dad is the size of a door
He's as cool as a freezer
But not as cool as me
Sometimes he tells me jokes
And they always make me laugh
He likes to read the paper.
That's my dad!

My dad likes to drink beer
And play football
And fix stuff like my toys
He's funny when we're playing games
And he's angry when he comes in from work
If we haven't changed out of our uniforms
He likes to go to the cinema with me
And he loves to watch 'Little Britain'.
That's my dad
And he's the best!

**Reece Ashmore (8)**
**Langbank Primary School, Langbank**


# Ice Is Nice

It's wintertime
Christmas is coming
Snowball fights together
Icicles hang high
The wind is whispering
All around
The snow falls softly
On your shoulders
Water turns to ice
The trees fall bare
Here and there
Children are
Happy because
Snow has fallen.

**Iain Gillon (10)**
**Langbank Primary School, Langbank**

# Through That Door

Through that door
Is the bottom of the ocean
Mermaids playing, fish swimming, stingrays gliding,
Sharks lurking in the shadows
*Suddenly*
Nets    s
          i
             n
               k
                 i
                   n
                     g
Sharks thinking, fish darting.

Reef emptied, complete silence,
Nothing stirring.

**Erin Kirsten Gilchrist  (7)**
**Langbank Primary School, Langbank**


# My Great Gran

My great gran died when I was four,
She used to smell of perfume and dust in a good way,
She had grey, short hair,
She was cuddlier than my gran at times,
She had blue eyes,
And she let me use her frame to make a spaceship in my game
And I was Luke Skywalker fighting Darth Vader,
She was covered in wrinkles,
And liked to say, 'Now eat all your dinner.'
She liked to sit in her favourite chair,
And had a nice tone of voice,
And always gave me a flavoured bonbon
Every time my mum was in the kitchen,
But now she's gone.

**Ciaran O'Neill  (9)**
**Langbank Primary School, Langbank**

# A Portrait Of Winter

He comes and makes it winter,
He makes the whole world white,
He comes when you are sleeping,
In bed, at midnight.

The children like to play with him,
Laughing in the snow,
They make snowmen out of him,
But they're sad when they have to go.

All the children have turkey,
Nobody is sad,
The children all are happy,
All things are good not bad.

You children all enjoy him,
You all sometimes sing,
He enjoys you playing with him,
And all the happiness he brings.

**Karen Sandeman (9)**
**Langbank Primary School, Langbank**


# A Portrait Of Winter

Looked out the window on a winter's day,
Saw some snow and went out to play,
It got a bit colder in the afternoon,
It started to rain, the snow will go soon.

Everyone has walked in the snow - *crush, crush*,
Now it's turning into slush,
It's too cold so you have to wear hats and mitts,
The council will soon come round with grit.

Finally the snow has gone,
You can now see the garden lawn,
Soon spring will be here,
And the rain will disappear.

**Lindsay Birch (9)**
**Langbank Primary School, Langbank**

# Through The Door

Through the door
There is a huge toy shop
With soft, cuddly toys
Lots of people are standing in a queue
Waiting to be served
Children are looking through the shelves
At all the little Beanie Babies
With smooth, small backs.

Mums and dads want to go home
But the boys and girls want to stay
The shopkeeper is counting out his money
And dropping it on the floor.

Everyone is talking about picnics and summer walks
But time is coming to an end
And we have to say goodbye.

**Naomi Hill  (8)**
**Langbank Primary School, Langbank**

# Through This Door

Through this door is ancient Egypt
Lots of pyramids standing tall
Slaves getting shouted at and getting whipped
The pharaoh going round in his solid gold chariot
The Nile flowing fast, the crops getting sown and harvested
But one more thing, it's really hot!

Through this door is a crumbling castle
It is full of ghosts, bats and skeletons in dungeons
Singing and dancing
But watch out, they might want to get you!

**Fraser Sweeney  (7)**
**Langbank Primary School, Langbank**

# The Doze

The Doze who lives behind the wall
The Doze who has grown extremely tall.
His soft, red and purple coat
Makes him very different from a goat.
Scary sounding,
But friendly, almost,
His only victim was his morning toast!

The Doze has two legs just like you and me,
His razor-sharp claws . . .
They couldn't harm a flea!

His yellow eyes improve his sight,
But on top of a building they scare him with the height!
At the sight of him villagers run a mile,
So going to town isn't worthwhile.
His head in the clouds, his feet down under,
So Australians believe his toes are like thunder!

His meals include yeast and self-raising flour,
Yet tall and colourful, he gains no power.
His best friend, a lime-green snail,
Although green, his face is pale.

The Doze, the snail, tall and small,
They live a happy life over the wall.

**Lynsey Mackay (11)**
**Langbank Primary School, Langbank**

# Through That Door

Through that door is a sweetie land
Waiting to be devoured
A chocolate milk pool
Awaits to be dipped in
Marshmallow seats and cotton candy pillows
Look as comfy as my bed
Everything is edible
Even the hard rock door
And if you are hungry
You can have even more
Tall, delicious gingerbread men
And Curly-Wurly stairs
Leading to sparkly-white Polo mint bangles
Or fruity Gummy Bears
Up another pair of yummy, swirly stairs
Where rainbow drops are falling on the super paper ground
And juicy jelly spiders crawling here and there
Sweetie Jelly Babies in their sticky honey cots
Crying their heads off just to get out
Along the sugar corridor
Is a scummy room filled with giant bubbles
Children chewing their teeth out with delicious bubblegum
Waiting for it to pop
If only this world would exist
Some day maybe, maybe not.

**Heather McFarlane (8)**
**Langbank Primary School, Langbank**

# Through This Door

Through that door is a treasure island
With waves splashing against rocks
Pirates approaching
They are looking for lots of gold
And necklaces

Through that door are sweeties and candy sticks
And gingerbread men
There are pillows made out of candyfloss, yum!
There are trees made out of lollipops

Through this door is Egypt
There are pyramids all over
There is pharaoh shouting at the slaves
Telling them, *get that, get this, feed me grapes*
Servants were really tired of all the work.

**Rebecca Mason (7)**
**Langbank Primary School, Langbank**


# My Furry Horse

I see a horse
I see it eating the grass
As well as eating I see it running
The colour is beautiful brown
I see the shape, it is very thin
The fur is very soft
The noise it makes is - *neigh!*
The other thing it does is take me riding
And goes to bed for a little snooze.

**Erin Lowrie (9)**
**Our Lady Of Peace Primary School, Linwood**

# I See A Hamster

I see a hamster
Running around the cage.
It is wiggling along the hay.
The colour of its skin is white.
It is round and fat
And furry and cuddly.
It squeaks like a mouse.
It runs around mad
And eats a lot.

**Shannon Deans (9)**
**Our Lady Of Peace Primary School, Linwood**


# Sharky The Goldfish

I see a goldfish
Swimming with bubbles coming out of its mouth
It's wagging its tail
Coloured in gold like rings
It's round like a rugby ball
Its scales are as smooth as fur
It goes *plop, plop, plop!*
It splashes water all over my face.

**Declan Barclay (9)**
**Our Lady Of Peace Primary School, Linwood**


# I See A Hamster

I see a hamster
Moving about very fast in his wheel
His colour is light brown and white
The noise he makes is a squeaking noise
He sleeps all day
He goes out at night
Every time I see him he is running about.

**Jay Cusack (9)**
**Our Lady Of Peace Primary School, Linwood**

# A Fat Dog

I see a dog
Licking its lips
Shuffling its feet
It's brown and black
With a big, fat body
With lots of fur
And a spotty back
The sound it makes
Is a barking noise
The other thing that it does
Is sniff its bum
With a big, black nose
And there it goes.

**Joseph Donnelly (9)**
**Our Lady Of Peace Primary School, Linwood**


# I See A Rabbit

I see a rabbit
Begging for its food
Buzzing up and down its little hutch
It's smooth
So beautiful and soft
Its body is long and big
Its colour is light orange
With a lovely white collar
It sneezes sometimes
And when I walk past
He jumps up to the cage.

**Calum Brawley (9)**
**Our Lady Of Peace Primary School, Linwood**

# A Fat Cat

I see a cat
A very fat cat
Who sits in a hat
It bites mice
It bites birds
It is black and white
A very fat cat
Which has short, spotty fur
*Miaow, miaow, miaow!*
It sleeps all day and all night
Off it strikes for another bird, *miaow!*

**Daniel Donnelly (9)**
**Our Lady Of Peace Primary School, Linwood**


# The Grizzly Dog

I see a dog
Staring straight at me
Waiting patiently
It is brown and black
And a wee bit white
It is kind of big and fat
Like a weasel
The fur is like a tennis ball
It growls like a grizzly bear
It buries quite a lot of bones
It runs straight at me and licks me.

**Scott Steedman (9)**
**Our Lady Of Peace Primary School, Linwood**

# I See A Cat

I see a cat
That likes to play
She is a black cat
Her body shape is round and small
She has fur that is smooth
She purrs and says, 'Miaow!'
She chases mice and birds
She likes staring at people
And she crawls in her bed.

**Lauren Fragapane  (9)**
**Our Lady Of Peace Primary School, Linwood**


# The Dog

I see a dog sitting
Waiting for a bone
It walks and it can also run fast
It is bright white
And it is kinda fat
It makes a noise like this - *woof, woof!*
It always chases its tail
And always eats flies all day long.

**Staci McDonald  (10)**
**Our Lady Of Peace Primary School, Linwood**


# I See A Sandy Dog

I see a dog
He's crying for his dinner
He moves very fast
He is sandy
He feels thin
The fur is soft
He growls a lot
He chases cats.

**Kayleigh Grant  (9)**
**Our Lady Of Peace Primary School, Linwood**

*Young Writers - Playground Poets Central Scotland*

# The Begging Dog

I see a dog
Sitting patiently waiting and begging for a bone
Putting his paw on my knee
His colour is brown
Mixed with black and cream
He is little
Making noises like he is trying to talk
Waiting and waiting
For a bone to chew on.

**Jack Main  (9)**
**Our Lady Of Peace Primary School, Linwood**


# The Sun

My day starts in the east
And ends in the west.
I go round the world in 24 hours.

You see me fly, I hurt your eye.
I shine your day, I wake you up.
I make your holiday worth going to.

*That's because I am the sun!*

**Cameron Byrne  (11)**
**Ravenswood Primary School, Cumbernauld**


# The Sunshine

I can cheer you up with my roasting delight
And give you a lovely tan.
I can bring you a smile and a cheery day.
But I can burn your skin because I am so bright.

**Mark Macdonald  (11)**
**Ravenswood Primary School, Cumbernauld**

# Harvest

Lots of autumn colours,
Brown, red, yellow and green.
Leaves flutter from trees up high,
Waiting to be gathered.

Farmers growing food to eat,
We share our harvest gifts.
Thinking of the poor and needy,
Giving thanks to God.

Squirrels scampering everywhere,
Gathering nuts and berries.
Owls sitting on branches so high,
Gazing into the midnight sky.

As the children come home for tea,
Hands full of conkers.
We hope they have time to think of God,
And spare some thoughts for others.

**Stacey Martin  (10)**
**Ravenswood Primary School, Cumbernauld**


## Harvest

Harvest is time to celebrate
With loads of laughter and glee.
Lots of conkers rolling about
Others picked up by me.

Autumn colours have arrived -
Red, orange, yellow, brown, green.
Leaves flutter from the trees
Some never to be seen.

Farmers are working in the fields
Finally sprouted the first crop.
Squirrels have gathered all their food
But now they have to stop.

**Leanna Marshall  (10)**
**Ravenswood Primary School, Cumbernauld**

# The Sun

I can burn and destroy and leave lands bare
I can come out to play and heat up the air.

I can be friendly or as mean as can be
I can give you a tan and warm up the sea.

When I am happy you can have lots of fun
But when I am angry then your life is done!

**Scott Flanagan (11)**
**Ravenswood Primary School, Cumbernauld**


# Harvest

H eaps of gold and orange leaves are dancing with the wind
A utumn leaves reveal their colours
R ed, crimson berries hang low from the tree
V elvet squirrels' tails are all that can be seen
E verlasting scarlet flowers bloom through all October
S mall, fluffy field mice run to hide from big machine
T owards the end the sunset comes to show an amber sky.

**Emma Wallace (11)**
**Ravenswood Primary School, Cumbernauld**


# Happiness

Happiness is light green
It smells like the fresh, spring air
It tastes like a lollipop
It sounds like the whistling of a jolly tune
It feels cool and breezy
Happiness lives behind the smile.

**Robyn Walker (10)**
**Ravenswood Primary School, Cumbernauld**

# Harvest

How I wonder what it would be like
To fly like a bird
Instead of riding my bike
I'd be up in the sky
Oh, what a beautiful sight
Although I'd hate to be flying
During the night.

I love all the colours, especially red
I stand in my room
And then like a leaf
I fall on my bed.

Squirrels are gathering their nuts
Rabbits are making their little huts
The frog in my pond
Moved to my front lawn.

All the butterflies
Fly up to the autumn skies
The flowers are growing
The farmers are sowing.

Oh, what a beautiful time of the year
Maybe instead of a bird
I could be a deer.

**Rachael Anderson  (10)**
**Ravenswood Primary School, Cumbernauld**


# Harvest

H arvest time is full of joy
A nd fairy-like leaves fluttering by
R eds and ambers, chestnuts and golds
V ast amounts of leaves glide to the ground
E ach squirrel stocks up for the winter
S outh fly the birds for the winter
T hanks are said in prayers to God.

**Jennifer Murray  (11)**
**Ravenswood Primary School, Cumbernauld**

# Up In The Attic

*(Based on 'Up In The Attic . . . Down In The Cellar . . .' by Wes Magee)*

and a bundle of books on the floor
standing is an old, haunted door
and a silver locket
pictures of a famous rocket
and on the floor is a squished bumblebee
there are spikes of a tree
up in the attic . . .

And . . . down in the cellar . . .
old Coke cans
bottle of fake tan
an old, old sheet
folded all neat
a dead, smelly rat
and a hungry cat.

**Aimee McGarragle (10)**
**Ravenswood Primary School, Cumbernauld**


# Up In The Attic . . . (And . . . Something's Stirring)

*(Based on 'Up In The Attic . . . Down In The Cellar . . .' by Wes Magee)*

Rusty, old painting sets
Old, green wellie boots
Rusty, old baby-grow
Dusty, old schoolwork
Dusty, old baby books
Old wedding photos

And . . . down in the cellar . . .
Rusty, old lawnmower
Old, silver bikes
Spiders in the cobwebby corners
Old, rusty scooters
Old, green watering can
Old plant pots.

**Chloé Patterson (10)**
**Ravenswood Primary School, Cumbernauld**

# Harvest

The bright, autumn colours
Red, yellow and green
And the grass covered, never to be seen.

In the autumn the leaves fall
And give thanks to the farmers
That share food with all.

Some evenings we have a sunset
Because usually this country is wet
So praise the Lord
The almighty one
Who makes the rain, wind and sun.

**Scott Campbell  (10)**
**Ravenswood Primary School, Cumbernauld**


# Four O'Clock Friday

Four o'clock Friday, I'm home at last,
Thinking the week has gone so fast.

On Monday when I went to school,
I went for lunch and got served gruel.

On Tuesday when I scored a goal,
I was so excited and dropped my roll.

On Wednesday I had got so stuck,
It looked like I was out of luck.

On Thursday I had passed the test,
I thought that mine was the best.

Four o'clock Friday, at last I'm free,
For two whole days no work for me.

**John McKenna  (11)**
**St Michael's Primary School, Parkhead**

# Days Of The Week

Monday sighed
Through the tiring day
Trying it keep itself awake
By hoisting its head off the desk
But failing every time

Tuesday tutted
In the buzzing classroom
Trying to avoid the teacher's glare
Not really thinking
Just being scared

Wednesday winked
During the exciting day
Swaggering along, telling everyone to get out of her way
Nobody arguing, just doing what they're told
She tried to be humble but had to be bold

Thursday snarled
Through the never-ending day
Dragging her bag behind her
Drawing pictures and writing sums
Trying to get on with the day

Friday chuckled
All the way through school
Laughing and cheering
In and out of classes
Being glad the week had ended.

**Kirsty McGowan  (11)**
**St Michael's Primary School, Parkhead**

# Days Of The Week

Monday howled
Through the exhausted school
Dragging the day along
Causing a lot of chaos
It huffed as it passed.

Tuesday screamed
Through the busy school
Making water bottles empty
Slamming stiff chairs
Waiting for the next challenge.

Wednesday skipped
Through the happy bunch
Putting smiles on faces
Producing very neat work
The day ended nicely.

Thursday danced
Through the cheerful school
Making life much better
Making work easier
Friday is nearly here.

Friday laughed
Through the excited school
No work needs doing
Fun time has begun
The weekend is near.

**Mark McGlynn  (12)**
**St Michael's Primary School, Parkhead**

# Days Of The Week

Monday sighed
Through the tiring day
Dragging her feet behind her
Opening books and homework
Staring, she grinned, as the three o'clock bell rang

Tuesday tutted
Through the enormous school
Opening doors with a warm welcome
Completing angles and 'English Alive' pages
Dreading the next day's challenges

Wednesday smiled
Through the exciting day
Making work easier and delighting teachers
Slowing pace down but don't worry
Friday's nearly here

Thursday laughed
Throughout the smiling class
Closing jotters and opening fun
Rushing their work like it'd never begun
Tomorrow is only a day away

Friday gazed
Throughout the ecstatic class
Making children joyful and well-behaved
Tidying tables and messing games
The weekend is nearly here.

**Danielle Finan  (11)**
**St Michael's Primary School, Parkhead**

# Days Of The Week

Monday mumbled
Through the yawning school
Dragging its bag along the ground
Banging trays and opening jotters
Sighing as it did its homework.

Tuesday tackled
The busy school
Searching for mapstart sheets to do
Opening textbooks and slamming doors
Then marking the homework jotters.

Wednesday worried
Throughout the tiring day
Sharpening pencils and doing tests
Making pencils write as fast as they can
But never allowing silence.

Thursday smiled
Through the cheerful school
Reading books and drawing pictures
Making jokes and playing games
And thinking, *only one day of school left.*

Friday laughed
Through the giggling school
Playing the computer and starting games
Dancing and singing songs
Then jumping out of school for the weekend.

**Adam Lindsay  (12)**
**St Michael's Primary School, Parkhead**

# Days Of The Week

Monday nagged
Throughout the classroom
Annoying the children
Keeping the weekend out
Opening the school week again

Tuesday spoke
As the school week began
Opening books
And sharpening pencils
Waiting for more work

Wednesday whistled
Over the smiling children
Opening text books
And empty jotters
Friday is nearly here

Thursday smiled
Through the happy school
Closing some text books
And workbook pages
Giggling and dancing

Friday laughed
As the weekend came
Closing all books
And mapstart pages
The weekend is here.

**Patrick Crichton  (11)**
**St Michael's Primary School, Parkhead**

# Days Of The Week

Monday sighed
As he staggered to school
Dragging his bag behind his tail
Waving slowly as he passed by.

Tuesday smirked
As he waited impatiently for Italian
He stomped down to tuck
Barging past everyone he meets.

Wednesday smiled
As he was first for lunch
She skipped into line
Laughing and joking at lunch.

Thursday laughed
As she did her work
Skipping outside to play with friends
Dancing quickly down the playground.

Friday sang
As she skipped joyfully to golden time
Playing games happily
As it was nearly home time.

**Hayley Braceland  (10)**
**St Michael's Primary School, Parkhead**

# Days Of The Week

Monday sighed
As the children groaned.
Can't wait till playtime
At least there's fun.

Tuesday moaned
As always.
Setting starts
And work begins.

Wednesday groaned
It isn't that fun
Without a thing to do
On a day like this.

Thursday giggled
We're nearly finished
The school week.
Can't wait till tomorrow.

Friday cheered
When school finished.
No more work
For a whole weekend.

**Shannon Rotchford  (10)**
**St Michael's Primary School, Parkhead**

# Personification Poetry

Summer giggled
Smiling down on the grass
Kissing children's faces
And lighting up the world.

Summer danced
Smiling down on the sweating beach
Tickling the laughing sea
And waving to the sand.

Summer kissed
The dancing plants
Cuddling the trees and leaves
Over the joyful park.

Summer sang
Over the smiling field
Cuddling the grazing pigs
Waiting for the grass to grow.

**Caitlin Cloherty (10)**
St Michael's Primary School, Parkhead


# Four O'Clock Friday

Four o'clock Friday, I'm home so fast,
Time to relax and forget about class.
On Monday at lunch they broke my toys,
They really are bad, bad boys.
On Tuesday afternoon at golden time,
They vandalised my bag and that's a crime.
On Wednesday they stood at the gate,
Then we started to have a debate.
On Thursday they laughed because I cried
When they stuck a pencil in my eye.
Four o'clock Friday, at last I'm free,
For two whole days they can't get me.

**Michael Halloran (11)**
St Michael's Primary School, Parkhead

# Summer

Summer sang
Down on the flowers
Kissing each child's face
And brightening up the sky

Summer laughed
Smiling on the trees
Shining on the leaves
And giving colour to the trees

Summer skipped
Over the sweating beach
Tickling the giggling sand
Waving to the sea

Summer danced
Over the joyful park
Kissing the grazing fields
As he passed with joy.

**Ryan Kennedy  (10)**
**St Michael's Primary School, Parkhead**


# My Friend

My friend is as quiet as a mouse
As sweet as sugar
She smells as beautiful as a rose
As a freshly-baked cake
My friend is as cute as a baby
As cuddly as a teddy bear
My friend's hair is as wavy as the sea
As black as coal
My friend's skin is as white as snow
As soft as a pillow
My friend is as kind as an angel
As caring as a mum.

**Danielle Whyte  (11)**
**St Michael's Primary School, Parkhead**

# Days Of The Week

Monday choked
Through the trembling school doors
Repeating what happens every single week
Massacring all the weekends
Trying to get through the week.

Tuesday stumbled
Into the creepy classroom
Opening the wrinkly books
And sharpening the crooked pencils
And eating time away.

Wednesday swaggered
Into the Antarctic gym
Stamping its feet and hitting its side
Wishing the day would sail by.

Thursday sprang
As Friday drew near
Closing revolting jotters
And chucking work tools aside
Putting the week at ease.

Friday emerged
As laughter spread all over the school like a plague
Brightness rose all above the classes
Playing games and having fun
This is the life for us.

**Megan Flynn (11)**
**St Michael's Primary School, Parkhead**

# Days Of The Week

Monday moaned
Through the yawning classroom
Pushing books open to find words
Listening at the clock go *tick-tock*
Creeping along after 3 o'clock

Tuesday screamed
In and out of the shouting classroom
Racing through the long corridors
Throwing rubbers in the air
Calming down as the day was nearly ended

Wednesday smiled
Through the working classroom
Playing and skipping
Eating lunch with a smile
The week was nearly through

Thursday laughed
Skipping on the way to school
Lighting up the day
Doing handwriting with a smile
As the weekend was near

Friday sang
Through the excited school
Jumping for joy for there was no homework
Golden time sheets flew around the school
Children ran out of school laughing
For it was the weekend.

**Samantha Watt (11)**
**St Michael's Primary School, Parkhead**

# Four O'Clock Friday

Four o'clock Friday, home at last,
I can't believe the week was so fast.
On Monday I won the quiz,
And was hailed as a real whiz.
On Tuesday I blasted the ball,
It was going in if the keeper wasn't so tall.
On Wednesday I beat the class,
Because I was the only one who got a pass.
On Thursday I felt so grand,
Because I was chosen to play in the school band.
Four o'clock Friday, that's me all done,
Now it's time for me to have some fun.

**Paul Campbell  (11)**
**St Michael's Primary School, Parkhead**


# Love

Love makes you feel like you're in Heaven
It is a great feeling until it is all over
And you feel as if your heart is broken
But it is just a phase that you go through
When you break up with someone really close to you
But your life will get better
And you might start dating if you're up to it.

**Sarah Green  (11)**
**St Thomas' Primary School, Neilston**


# Stilian Petrov

I see him scoring magnificent goals
I hear him screaming when he gets tackled badly
I smell his sweat after a game
I taste the water that he drinks at half-time
I feel brilliant when he scores a goal.

**Jordan Allan  (9)**
**St Thomas' Primary School, Neilston**

# He Is My Pet

I had a dog,
He was very happy.
I liked to call him
Captain Fatty!

He wasn't tatty,
Although he was happy.
He ate my other pet
Called Mr Catty!

I missed my cat,
But the dog is better.
I wrote all about them
In a letter!

My dog is my pet
That hates the vet.
He gives him jabs,
And my dog plays with bags!

**Neil Joseph Morran (9)**
**St Thomas' Primary School, Neilston**

# Spring

Warm fingers, warm toes.
Sitting down where the flowers grow.
Play in the garden, skipping along.
Happy toes, my toes are warm.
When the birds are humming in the breeze
It's like music from the trees.
When I get ice cream my teeth are cold,
My ears are cold, my hands are warm.
I put my hands over my ears.
My ears are warm.

**Sarah Aird (8)**
**St Thomas' Primary School, Neilston**

# Pets

My pet is blue as a bell
And her name is Bluebell.
She flies really high.
She's the colour of the sky.
Her little sister died
And she was the first that flied.
Sometimes she crashes
And sometimes she bashes.
Her beak was almost bleeding.
She does a lot of feeding.
She's really, really fat.
She's wanted by the cat
Who likes to wear a hat.
She sleeps a lot
And baths a lot
And that is that.

**Jasmine Kennedy (8)**
**St Thomas' Primary School, Neilston**


# Spring

What was once dead is now alive
For the colour of spring makes it alive
Everything is light, everything is growing
For you will never see it snowing
The trees are bright, even at night
They will shine
For the song of spring has a spark
A spark of brightness and colour
For the light glows through the season.

**Adam Nicholson (8)**
**St Thomas' Primary School, Neilston**

# Favourite Things

Everyone likes different things.
Everyone has a favourite thing.
What is mine? What is yours?
It might even be seaside shores.
Butterflies, flutterflies.
Made up things, fluffy things.
Green trees and yellow bees.
Yellow cheese and green peas.
Spotty dresses, blue messes.
Ice cream cones and doggy bones.
Toy cars, twinkling stars.
Chocolate bars and planet Mars.
Things to eat, stamping feet.
Coloured pens, fat hens.
Best friends, dead ends.
Grey tellies, red jellies.
Brown sheds and warm beds.

**Nadine Gallagher  (8)**
**St Thomas' Primary School, Neilston**


# Seasons, Seasons

Spring, spring, glorious spring
Listening to the chirping birds.

Summer, summer, warm as fire,
As it's fun when playing in the sun.

Autumn, autumn, changing colours,
Leaves falling off trees.

Winter, winter, wrap up warm,
Let's go out to play in the snow.

**Adam Martin  (9)**
**St Thomas' Primary School, Neilston**

# Winter Nights

W inter skies
I cy snow
N ice, warm beds
T rees frozen
E arly morning
R obins cheeping

N ice, warm homes
I cy nose
G irls chatting
H orses chanting
T icking clock

    I love winter nights.

**Kirsty Lappin (8)**
**St Thomas' Primary School, Neilston**


# Winter Nights

W arm rooms
I cy ponds
N ests frozen
T rees frozen
E veryone playing
R obins running

N umb fingers
I cy toes
G irls laughing
H ouses all warm
T rees blowing
S now falling

I love winter nights.

**Amber Fleming (8)**
**St Thomas' Primary School, Neilston**

# Winter Nights

W arm bed
I cy puddles
N ests frozen
T rees frozen
E arly mornings
R obins tweeting

N ights warm
I cy toes
G irls playing
H ouses cosy
T weeting birds
S now falling

I love winter nights.

**Rheagan Dougall  (8)**
**St Thomas' Primary School, Neilston**


# Winter Nights

W indy nights
I cy puddles
N umb fingers
T oes numbing
E arly nights
R obins singing

N ests frozen
I cy leaves
G iant icicles
H igh, snowy hills
T umbling snow
S liding down the snow.

**Lauren Diamond  (8)**
**St Thomas' Primary School, Neilston**

## My Favourite Things

F lowers are so lovely
L ovely is what I say
O range, yellow, any colour
W here they are is way away
E very day I see them, they are so nice
R obins see them also
S o you better look out.

I like flowers.

**Heather Gough  (8)**
St Thomas' Primary School, Neilston


## Spring

S is for song, the song of a bird.
P is for petals of daffodil flowers.
R is for rabbits popping up in surprise.
 I is for insects, ladybirds and flies.
N is for nests the birds make fast.
G is for garden, big and warm.

Spring! Spring! Oh, what a beautiful thing!

**Holly McLaughlin  (8)**
St Thomas' Primary School, Neilston


## Spring

S pring is a lovely time of year.
P eople having fun.
R ound the world people rejoice.
 I t is a lovely time of year.
N ow it is spring and baby animals are born.
G oing out is so much fun, that's why I love spring.

**Kerry McMahon  (8)**
St Thomas' Primary School, Neilston

# Me And My Friends

On a lovely, sunny day,
My friends and I go out to play.

Football is what we play,
All through the lovely, sunny day.

Tomorrow is another sunny day,
So we will play just like yesterday!

**Jordan Whiteford  (9)**
St Thomas' Primary School, Neilston


# Summer

Summer is my favourite season
When lovely birds start to cheep
And flowers dance in the breeze
Bumblebees flying through the trees
Paddling pools are out today
Some people just want to play.

**Louisa Kearney  (8)**
St Thomas' Primary School, Neilston


# Favourite Things

Ice cream and chocolate are my favourite things
Lollies and teddies are so cute
They are so fluffy and nice
Reading and working
That is what I like.
These are some of my favourite things.

**Blair Martin  (8)**
St Thomas' Primary School, Neilston

# My Favourite

Ice skate
Fishing bait
Brother skates
They shake
Winter wheels
Dogs' heels
Shiny vase
Shiny car
Shiny model
Intense ride
Lovely house
Big mouse
Slidy ice
Really care
My lair
Shiny hideout
Sugary sweets
Lovely treats
Lucky clover
Shiny boulder.

**Declan Wylie  (8)**
**St Thomas' Primary School, Neilston**


# Me

I am Stuart, I'm no fool
I would say I'm rather cool
I like cars, I like money
I would say I'm rather funny
I have a family, I have a heart
I would say I'm rather smart
I have friends and a family
I have hands, I have feet
I would say my life is complete.

**Stuart Gough  (11)**
**St Thomas' Primary School, Neilston**

# Money, Money, Money

There is money to steal
And you can't get a meal
The things that you feel
Can always be healed

The money is real
The secret is sealed
The money we'll shield
From the people who steal

The emotions that you feel
Might not earn you a deal
But try not to steal
Or you won't manage to heal.

**Cameron Coyne  (11)**
**St Thomas' Primary School, Neilston**


# The Stars At Night

I look out my window
Up to the darkness above
There is a flicker of light
That makes it look bright
A slight sparkle flashing up
In the air
It makes the darkness of the night
Seem to glare
This is a star
A creature of the night
Above in the sky
Making it alight.

**Mark Docherty  (11)**
**St Thomas' Primary School, Neilston**

# Favourite Things

I *see* the boys playing football
I *hear* the crowd shout
I *smell* the muck coming off the players' shoes
I *taste* the nice hot dogs from the stands
I *feel* like we have won the World Cup.

**David John Dunn (10)**
St Thomas' Primary School, Neilston

# Zak's Haiku

He is black and white.
Come and throw his big, red ball.
Zak loves his warm fire.

**Craig Doherty (10)**
St Thomas' Primary School, Neilston

# Cats Haiku

Cats are beautiful.
I am glad I keep them all.
They are furry friends.

**John-Gerard Shepherd (10)**
St Thomas' Primary School, Neilston

# My Dog's Haiku

Dogs are fun and warm.
I take them on walks each day.
I have two of them.

**John Aird (10)**
St Thomas' Primary School, Neilston

# Scotland

Scotland has many hills and mountains
It's my favourite country ever
It sometimes has bad weather
But that's okay for me
Scotland is so beautiful
Its people are so nice
And that's good enough for me
That's why I adore Scotland.

**Liam Morran (11)**
St Thomas' Primary School, Neilston

# Down On The Beach

Down on the beach,
Sitting on the warm sand,
Watching people laugh and play.

Down on the beach,
Swimming in the sea,
And splashing all through the day.

**Kendle Keenan (9)**
St Thomas' Primary School, Neilston

# My Favourite Things

My favourite things are all around
But some places they are not to be found
The sweets, the juice, the toys I adore
After I get it I always want more
I know I can't get it all
But I still stay standing tall
Now all that I have I get at the mall.

**Dominique Drinnan (11)**
St Thomas' Primary School, Neilston

# Winter

Winter is a season of love and joy,
Something under the tree for every girl and boy.

Up in the sky I see a sleigh,
Santa Claus is on his way.

Rudolph, Comet and Cupid too,
Helping to bring a present to you.

Turkey, potatoes and Brussels sprouts,
Heating up a family's house.

Children playing on their sleigh,
Winter really makes your day.

With all that joy that winter does bring,
It's almost sad to move to spring.

**Gareth Toner  (10)**
**St Thomas' Primary School, Neilston**


# Holiday

I *see* the gleaming ocean and the sparkling beach too.
I *hear* the children playing in the waves and in the sunshine.
I *smell* the nice food from the cafés at lunchtime.
I *taste* the salt when I go for a dip.
I *feel* the sand between my toes.

**Mhairi Hannigan  (10)**
**St Thomas' Primary School, Neilston**


# My Pet Budgie

I see my pet budgie creeping on my shoulder,
I smell my pet budgie eating its dinner,
I hear my pet budgie making chirping sounds,
I feel my pet budgie crawling on my head,
My pet budgie is my favourite pet.

**Aidan John Reid  (9)**
**St Thomas' Primary School, Neilston**

# The Simpsons

The Simpsons is my favourite show
With Homer, Marge, Maggie and Moe
Mr Burns with an evil plan, he really is a nasty man
Their neighbour Flanders, he loves God
But sadly he's got a dead wife Maude
Seymour Skinner loves to teach
Like Reverend Lovejoy loves to preach
Professor Frink tries to think of ingenious inventions
There's Carl who's best friends with Lenny
And there's Lisa who's best friends with Jenny
There's Jub-Jub eating his grub-grub
Driving Patty batty
Barney Gumble drinking at Moe's
Captain McCallistar shouting, 'Thar he blows!'
There's Marge with her large hairdo
Big, bold and very blue
They've been through many antics
Like meeting Tony Blair
And being attacked by a grizzly bear
Yes, The Simpsons is my favourite show
But now, friends, it's time to go.

**Anton Queen (11)**
St Thomas' Primary School, Neilston


# Lenny The Green Beetle

My mum has a green Beetle called Lenny
And a green Mini called Benny
It drives about the village and it shines with pride
'That must be the green Beetle!' the people shout
It wouldn't hurt a fly and when it goes by
The people shout, 'It's Wendy in the Beetle!'
There are many silver, blue, black and green Beetles
But Lenny's the best Beetle ever!

**Claire Walker (11)**
St Thomas' Primary School, Neilston

# Flying

Flying, flying seems so much fun,
But don't get too close to the sun.
Icarus tried it but did not succeed,
But that's just a legend of the Greeks.
I want to fly up so high,
Right into the big, blue sky.
I want to see the people below,
Then fly down and say hello.
The only way that I can fly,
Is in a plane up in the sky.
It's not fair, birds can fly,
So why can't I?

**Rebecca Lees (11)**
**St Thomas' Primary School, Neilston**


# My Holiday

Having lots of fun in the water,
Having lots of fun in the sand as well.
Laughing at my brother's dive,
Laughing at the seagulls fly.
Enjoying my cold ice cream,
Enjoying being on *holiday!*

**Adam Forde (9)**
**St Thomas' Primary School, Neilston**


# Spring

I see flowers in spring,
I smell lovely fresh air in spring,
I hear birds singing in spring,
I taste ice cream in spring,
I touch fluffy lambs in spring.

**Harry Hogan (10)**
**St Thomas' Primary School, Neilston**

# Me And My Friends

On a lovely, sunny day,
Me and my friends go out to play.
We all take out our chocolate buns,
And have lots and lots of fun.

We all play football on the pitch,
But normally the ball
Falls in the ditch.

We all go in at nine o'clock,
And remember to set our alarm clocks.
Tomorrow just the same,
It's a sunny day,
And we all go back out to play!

**Matthew Gallanagh  (9)**
**St Thomas' Primary School, Neilston**

# School

School, school, working at school,
Some think it's not good
And some think it's cool.
The work, the teachers, the staff
And the friends,
I'm always relieved
When the school finally ends.
What is the meaning of going to school?
It's the education and art is quite cool.
Seeing your friends and your teachers as well,
Going to the nurse when you're not feeling well.
So if I had to comment on going to school,
The thing that I'd say is school is quite cool.

**Marianne Gallanagh  (11)**
**St Thomas' Primary School, Neilston**

# My Summer Holiday

H appy holidays here again,
O n the plane flying away.
L ollipops and ice cream in my hand,
I n the pool where it is cold and fun.
D ay by day the holidays go by,
A t the beach laughing.
Y awning in the summer sun.
S wimming, playing and singing as well!

**Katie Mackenzie (9)**
St Thomas' Primary School, Neilston

# Holidays

H appy times
O n the sand,
L ying in the sun.
I n the sea,
D eep as can be.
A nd waves push you around.
Y oung children playing.
S o much fun on holidays!

**Megan McCarron (9)**
St Thomas' Primary School, Neilston

# A Friend

There's nothing more important to me than a friend
They will stick by you from start to end.
When you are feeling so lonely, so sad
They'll cheer you up and you will be glad.
When you fall anywhere in the land
They will come over and give you a hand.
When your face is filled with tears
They will say something to fill you with cheers.

**Jack Mayberry (11)**
St Thomas' Primary School, Neilston

# The Four Seasons

*Spring* is when the bulbs push through the earth
And the flowers begin to grow
Out comes the sun and away goes the snow
Lambs struggle to stand on all fours
And how beautifully the birds in the sky soar
The grass and leaves begin to turn green
And all these things in spring are seen.

*Summer* is when the sun shines bright
People relax and no school in sight
Sunglasses, lotion is what we use
So we don't burn and go bright rouge!
We enjoy *summer* because it is fun
And we all like to soak up the sun.

*Autumn* is when the leaves turn brown
All of them usually end up on the ground
The chestnuts have a spiky, green shell
We crack them to get the brown conker inside
It gets a bit colder and the wildlife start hibernating
*Winter* is coming, we start preparing.

Hats and scarves are what we wear
When the cold *winter* is here
The snow starts to fall and the temperatures drop
All the hot weather suddenly stops
*Winter* starts to end and we know what's round the bend
We prepare for all the four seasons to come all over again.

**Amy Smith (11)**
**St Thomas' Primary School, Neilston**


# All About Me

My hair is blonde, my eyes are blue
I have some freckles and wear pigtails
I like to play and eat ice cream
And like to shop non-stop
I also like to be exactly like me!

**Melissa Linda McGlinchey (11)**
**St Thomas' Primary School, Neilston**

# Maltesers

The circular chocolatey, sugary treat
Fills me up right down to my feet.
The feeling inside from this wonderful crunch
Makes me continue this marvellous munch.
The honeycomb, bubbly taste is just right
It is a great sweet, it's my delight.
No one knows just what I mean
When I say the taste is extreme.
Maltesers are my number one dream.
Maltesers are the best
Better than all the rest.

**Dennis Sweenie  (11)**
**St Thomas' Primary School, Neilston**


# The Fox And The Owl

Through the window, past the trees
There is a fox and owl staring at me
Their eyes are very bright
Just like the stars that shine at night
But they make no sound at all
The owl flies from tree to tree
As the fox still stares at me
And when the snow is falling
It freezes the grass
As I turn around
The owl flies past.

**Susanne Wallace  (11)**
**St Thomas' Primary School, Neilston**

# My Best Friend Is Nad

Iona sits and stares
Steven scribbles like mad
I want the best idea I've ever had
So the teacher isn't always sad

Liam Feeney drives me mad
Nicole Craig is very bad
My best friend is Nad
When we're together I'm very glad

At the playground
We all play
Happy each and every single day
In we go every day.

**Christopher Allen  (11)**
**St Timothy's Primary School, Greenfield**


# In The Morning

My alarm goes off at half-past seven
When I'm usually lying in dream heaven
I then get dressed in my uniform
I have to look in top form!
For breakfast maybe I'll have a waffle
With melting jam of which I gobble!
My face washed, my hair brushed
Toothbrush in mouth and all is a-hush!
Then I have to walk my dog
Possibly be dragged through a bog!
It's then time to go to school
I keep attending so as not to be a fool!

**Iona May  (11)**
**St Timothy's Primary School, Greenfield**

# Brave Gelert

I see the Prince Gelert and the baby
I hear the baby gurgling and the prince laughing
I smell the baby and dinner cooking
I feel everyone is happy

I see great bravery
I hear snarling and growling
I smell fear
I feel scared

I see anger
I hear silence
I smell blood
I feel shock

I see sudden spurts of blood
I hear fierce stabbing
I smell horror
I feel tension

I see Gelert dying
I hear the baby crying
I smell death
I feel great sadness.

**Kieran Gibbens  (9)**
**St Timothy's Primary School, Greenfield**


# Brothers!

Brothers smell
Brothers tell
I think they should clean themselves
One day they might hurtle down a well
Because of my evil sister's spell!
*Ha, ha, ha!*

**Laura Henaghen  (11)**
**St Timothy's Primary School, Greenfield**

# When I Go Back To School

When I go to school
I find it really boring
And in the afternoon
I hear people snoring

I won a competition
In a club one day
When my dad goes to the pub
I shout, *'Hooray!'*

When I am in the playground
I run about all day
When they shout at me
I say, 'Go away.'

Now school's over
I think everything's done
Then I go about mad
Starting to run.

**Shannon Love  (11)**
**St Timothy's Primary School, Greenfield**


# Friday Football Fun

Friday football fun,
Warming up and exercises,
Always on the run.

Goalkeepers, defenders, midfielders, strikers too,
Constantly passing and shooting,
If you're not fast they'll catch you.

Football is great,
Keepy-ups, sit-ups, press-ups,
If you wear the number eight.

**James Reynolds  (11)**
**St Timothy's Primary School, Greenfield**

# Animals

A n elephant is rather big,
N aughty dogs shall always dig,
I nside pets that you'll have to train,
M any cats hate the rain,
A ll animals I'll always love,
L ots of people will love a dove.
S mall mice somehow will get in your house.

**Hannah Neilson  (11)**
**St Timothy's Primary School, Greenfield**

# Summer

S ummertime is very warm
U nless you get a big storm
M any people going out to play
M any things we have to say
E very evening we hide down a lane
R unning and hiding until we get rain.

**Steven Slane  (9)**
**St Timothy's Primary School, Greenfield**

# School

'S sshhh,' says the teacher from the end of the class
C alling our names out from the list
H ow she always makes me shiver
O h and the awful smell of her breath
O f coffee, I hate that
'L ate again!' she shouts at me.

**Chloe O'Donnell  (11)**
**St Timothy's Primary School, Greenfield**

# Why I Love Scotland

S cotland is the best
C ome and have a look
O r read about it in a book
T ourists come to Edinburgh to
L ook at the castle and its glory
A lways questions
N ever-ending story
D o you want to come to Scotland?

**Kieran Regan  (11)**
St Timothy's Primary School, Greenfield

# My Team Celtic

C eltic are so amazing
E very other team is no good
L iverpool thought they were great
T ill Celtic beat them by eight
I think Celtic have the best fans
'C ause the supporters travel the land.

**Anthony Canning  (11)**
St Timothy's Primary School, Greenfield

# Celtic

C eltic is the team for me
E very Saturday I am there in the stand
L eague championship will be ours 2004-2005
T here, in the sun, Celtic holding the cup
I can hardly believe my joy
C eltic are the best team *ever!*

**Chantelle McMillan  (11)**
St Timothy's Primary School, Greenfield

## St Timothy's School Is The Best

St Timothy's school is so cool
Even though it has no pool
Something for everyone, outings are good
Every day I want to stay, anyone would
The teachers are so nice
Miss McCamley wrote a poem about head lice
St Timothy's school is so cool
The place where nobody is a fool.

**Pauline Clark  (11)**
**St Timothy's Primary School, Greenfield**


## My Best Friend

My best friend is really pretty
She is also very witty
We met each other in primary one
Every day we play and have fun
We always hang around together
Hopefully we'll be friends forever!

**Kayleigh McGuirk  (11)**
**St Timothy's Primary School, Greenfield**


## Limerick

There was an old man from Fife,
Who somehow hated his life,
He jumped out his bed,
And got a bang on the head,
And he had to be nursed by his wife!

**Michael McCann  (11)**
**St Timothy's Primary School, Greenfield**

# Football Frenzy

When I play football I run about mad
Every day I'm crazy
I feel very bad.

When I scored a goal
I thought it was really cool
I bought a camera
But it ran out of spool.

When my mum comes to my games
I get really nervous
When my team scores a goal
I feel impervious.

**Kierron McArthur (11)**
**St Timothy's Primary School, Greenfield**


# My Family

My family are so mad
I am really very glad
My sister Kayleigh has hair that is brown
And constantly she wears a great frown
Lind's my mum and she's never glum
And my dad Gerry is always merry.

**Carly Docherty (11)**
**St Timothy's Primary School, Greenfield**


# There Was An Old Man From Dundee

There was an old man from Dundee
Who was very fond of iced tea
So after one glass
He'd roll on the grass
And run about shouting, 'I'm free!'

**Kieran Donaldson (11)**
**St Timothy's Primary School, Greenfield**

# Brave Gelert

I see peace and beauty
I hear birds twittering
I smell the baby and I feel calm

I see blood and horror
I hear ripping
I smell wolves and I feel hurt

I see horror and blood spurting
I hear dog growling
I smell stench of blood and I feel furious

I see sleeping and silence
I hear baby breathing
I smell flesh and I feel angry

I see a dog dying and yelping
I hear stillness
I smell dying and
I feel confused.

**Ryan Clifford  (11)**
**St Timothy's Primary School, Greenfield**


# Worry

Worry is white,
It sounds like chalk
Scraping on the blackboard.
It tastes like hard sea salt
Freshly found at sea.
It smells like a dead mouse
That a cat was playing with earlier that morning.
It looks like rush hour traffic
On the motorway.
It feels like people jagging pins
In your side.
It reminds me of someone in a trap
Struggling to get out.

**Chloe Anne White  (10)**
**Scotstoun Primary School, Scotstoun**

# Anger

Anger is red like a bull charging
It sounds like a bomb exploding inside me
And it tastes like having a drink of blood
It smells like a fire burning a house
Anger looks like a ferocious bulldog
And it feels as rugged and spiky as wood
It reminds me of a wild boar running crazy.

**Alexander Calderwood (10)**
**Scotstoun Primary School, Scotstoun**


# Anger

Anger is black like the darkness in the night,
It sounds like a volcano erupting
And it tastes like flowing lava going down a volcano.
Anger smells like a fire burning inside of me,
It looks like a cheetah about to pounce on its prey
And it smells like a body rotting in the sewer.
It reminds me of my dad going mad.

**Andrew Hardie (10)**
**Scotstoun Primary School, Scotstoun**


# Terror

Terror is black like a pitch-dark night,
It sounds like thunder raving in the sky
And tastes like raw meat as a shark's dinner.
Terror smells like burning rubber in a bonfire,
It looks like a zombie coming towards me
And feels like the Grim Reaper touching me.
It reminds me of a fire-breathing dragon.

**Conor Clements (10)**
**Scotstoun Primary School, Scotstoun**

# Happy!

Happy is yellow like a lovely sun in the sky.
It sounds like a newborn baby crying.
It tastes like roses falling from the sky.
It smells like ice cream and jelly.
It looks like people rolling in the grass.
It feels like hugging your teddy bear.
It reminds me of laughing and having fun together.

**Rachel Turner  (10)**
Scotstoun Primary School, Scotstoun


# Happy Times

Happiness is yellow like a sunflower
It sounds like angels singing
And tastes like chocolate and strawberry milkshakes
It smells like roses
It looks like a rainbow
And feels like waves hitting me in the sea
It reminds me of my birthday.

**Raymond Robertson  (10)**
Scotstoun Primary School, Scotstoun


# Anger

Anger is the colour of red
It tastes like hot peppers
Anger sounds like drums
And it smells like smoke
Anger looks like the Devil
It feels like my soul's gone
Anger reminds me of death.

**Kieran Stewart  (10)**
Scotstoun Primary School, Scotstoun

# I'm Bored

I'm really bored,
There's nothing to do,
It's a rainy day,
So I can't go out to play.
All my friends are on holiday,
I don't even have any homework to do,
Old man Shoonty is babysitting me,
He's such a bore.
Boredom is really grey,
It sounds like a quiet wind passing by.
It tastes like water without any flavour,
It feels like rough rock.
It smells like dust.
Boredom looks like nothing,
Just a blank space at the end of the world.
It reminds me of an empty room with nothing in it.
I really hate being *bored!*

**Eilidh Anne Macleod  (10)**
Scotstoun Primary School, Scotstoun


# Anger

Anger is red, more red that blood
And hotter than fire
It sounds like wolves howling at the moon
And tastes like evil and bad
It smells like gloom and sadness
It looks like two Doberman dogs fighting
It feels like fire burning your face
It reminds me of hate and death.

**Megan Wilkie  (10)**
Scotstoun Primary School, Scotstoun

# Love

Love is romantic like the red, red rose.
Love sounds like a heart thumping madly.
It tastes like sweet chocolate fudge cake
With dribbling cream.
Love smells like a fresh, summer's day
Waking up with the biggest smile on your face.
Love looks like a poppy beaming as red as a love heart.
Love feels like a soft cloud
As white as snow, breaking up gently as I touch it.
Love reminds me of a teddy bear
Cuddling you when you need love.

**Megan Auld (10)**
Scotstoun Primary School, Scotstoun


# The Madness Within

Madness is scarlet-red like a tiger's mouth after its daily meal,
It sounds like a tornado destroying everything in its path
And it tastes like coal turned white with heat.
It smells like toxic smoke poisoning everything it passes,
It looks like lava spreading like wild fire
And feels like acid burning all of my organs.
It reminds me of lions ripping up a warthog
As if it were nothing but a toy.

**Lauren Walsh (10)**
Scotstoun Primary School, Scotstoun


# Embarrassment

Embarrassment is as pink as a flamingo.
It sounds like a hyena laughing in Hell.
It tastes like catarrh in your mouth.
It smells like pigs in a shed
And feels like you're sinking into sand.
It reminds me of going to school with no trousers on.

**Amy Maclellan (10)**
Scotstoun Primary School, Scotstoun

# Happiness

Happy is blue and yellow
Like the sun and the sky.
It sounds like birds singing in the trees
And it tastes like ice cream
With raspberry and chocolate sprinkles on it.
It smells like air freshener inside of me.
It feels like people rolling in the flowers
And it reminds me of people being friends.

**John-Ross Rennie (10)**
Scotstoun Primary School, Scotstoun


# Sadness Is Sad

Sadness is blue like the ocean swallowing me in.
It sounds like parents shouting at me
And it tastes like a plant as sour as can be.
It smells like seaweed whirling around me.
It looks like the ocean filled with my tears
And feels like needles going right through me.
Sadness reminds me of a pack of wolves tearing me apart.

**Eilidh Fletcher (10)**
Scotstoun Primary School, Scotstoun


# Envy

Envy is green as a poisonous plant looking for its prey.
It sounds like a screeching baby hungry for food.
It tastes rotten and horrible as polluted water.
It smells like dirt and mud
And stinks as much as a body rotting in Hell.
It looks like a swamp with a crocodile waiting for someone to kill.
It feels pointy, grumpy and sour inside.
It reminds me of people showing off their things and not sharing.

**Conor Mellish (10)**
Scotstoun Primary School, Scotstoun

# Hot Head

Anger is blood, it feels like murder in the street
It sounds like people shouting and screaming
And it tastes of burning pitch ashes
And salty, turquoise sea.
I smell it and it smells of out of date cheese.
I see it and it looks like people eating chillies
And gasping for water.
It feels like kids spray painting on buildings.
It reminds me of ashes falling from the ceiling.

**Matthew Mouat (10)**
**Scotstoun Primary School, Scotstoun**


# Terror Is Terrifying!

Terror is white as fear itself,
It sounds like somebody's screaming
While being bitten by a vampire.
It tastes like dirt, it's that horrible.
Terror smells like a dead body crawling out of its grave.
It very much looks like a pterodactyl just before it rips my head off.
It feels like a spirit taking over my body.
Terror always reminds me of my head teacher.

**Jay Jenkins (10)**
**Scotstoun Primary School, Scotstoun**


# Fear

Fear is black like a pitch-black forest.
It sounds like a person struggling to get out.
Fear tastes like rotten blood dripping in my mouth.
It smells like vile, dead bodies.
Fear looks like a pack of hungry wolves ripping apart a deer.
It feels like red-backed spiders crawling on me.
It reminds me of a teacher turning into a goblin
And eating me alive - *slowly!*

**Callum McDonald (10)**
**Scotstoun Primary School, Scotstoun**

# Why? Why? Why?

Why do you have to change shoes?
Because you need special shoes to play bowling.
Why do you have to bowl with a ball?
Because if you did it with a square one it wouldn't roll.
Why are these skittles at the end of the lane?
Because you have to knock them down, it's the aim of the game.
Why can't you go over the red line?
Because if you did you'd be cheating.
Why is a strike so good?
*Because it's the best score*
    Keep breathing, 1 . . . 2 . . . 3

Ahh! Why is it called bowling?
Because you bowl balls . . .
What colour are your shoes?
*Be quiet!*

*Why?*

**Nicole Follen  (9)**
**Thorntree Primary School, Glasgow**


# Walking To School On A Rainy Morning

The rainbow shone across the school
The rain came splashing like a fool
I had to dash and saw a splash
And then became like someone cool

The sun shone up, the rain came down
And then my heart became a beating sound
I ran into school like a fool
And after school I went to the town.

**Stephen Wells  (10)**
**Thorntree Primary School, Glasgow**

# The River

The river is like a calm glass of water sparkling in the sun.
I'm sitting by the old, oak tree
Watching the wind calmly blow the river.
Down the road it's like the glass is tipping over.
I am on my way home now,
Here comes a gust of wind.
Now it's like the river's waving goodbye
Because I'm going home.
I would say bye-bye now and turn away.
The end of the road taking me home.
There is no water, no river.
Walking home not so glad.
I might not see the river again,
It makes me sad.

**Karyn Ross  (9)**
**Thorntree Primary School, Glasgow**


# Joe

There once was a boy called Joe
Who had a big sore toe
He woke to find
He'd lost his mind
And didn't even know!

**John Sneddon  (10)**
**Thorntree Primary School, Glasgow**


# Untitled

There once was a boy named Paul
Who bumped into a very large wall
He got a sore head
So he went to his bed
And that's how stupid was Paul.

**Roxanne Wright  (10)**
**Thorntree Primary School, Glasgow**

# Love

I am red like roses.
I taste like sweet candyfloss.
I smell of fresh air.
I look like secrets.
I sound like sweet chat.
I feel lovely and warm.

I am love.

**Amy Higgins  (10)**
**Thorntree Primary School, Glasgow**


# Happy

The colour is like baby-blue
The taste is like a twister ice lolly
The smell is like a rose
The look is like babies playing
The sound is birds singing
The feel is soft cotton wool
I am happy.

**Nicole McIntosh  (10)**
**Thorntree Primary School, Glasgow**


# Red

My colour is red
My taste is bitter
I smell like fire
I look like a roaring bear
I sound like an earthquake
I feel like a volcano

I am anger.

**Kyle Harris  (10)**
**Thorntree Primary School, Glasgow**

# Fairground!

F un at the fairground
A nd the ice cream is lovely
I love the Mexican Mayhem
R ound and round on the big wheel
G host train is fun
R ound and round all the rides
O verall the people in the fair
U nder the water
N o better than the fairground
D ash! I need to go!

**James Paterson  (9)**
**Thorntree Primary School, Glasgow**


# A Bomb Is Coming

A bomb is coming for the town
It's really, really coming close down
So really, go away
Come back another day
Then please be back
Before it takes the crown.

**Daniel Melrose  (10)**
**Thorntree Primary School, Glasgow**


# Ali

There was a little girl called Ali
Who wanted to play in a rally
She dreamed to win
Woke up in a bin
And never won the rally.

**Ali Sedgwick  (10)**
**Thorntree Primary School, Glasgow**

# The Amazing Star

The amazing star
I saw it shine from afar
It was shining bright
So full of light
It was easy to see
It has to be
The best star of all
So big but yet so small
I wish I knew
How I would get two
Of my amazing stars
That shone from afar.

**Kimberley McCarron  (10)**
**Thorntree Primary School, Glasgow**